W9-ADS-830

Sexual Power in British Romantic Poetry

Sexual Power in British Romantic Poetry

Daniel P. Watkins

University Press of Florida

Gainesville/Tallahassee/Tampa/Boca Raton
Pensacola/Orlando/Miami/Jacksonville

01 00 99 98 97 96   6 5 4 3 2 1

Library of Congress Cataloging-in-Publication Data
Watkins, Daniel P., 1952-
Sexual power in British romantic poetry / Daniel P. Watkins.
    p. cm.
Includes bibliographical references and index.
ISBN 0-8130-1438-7 (alk. paper)
1. English poetry—19th century—History and criticism. 2. Wordsworth,
William, 1770-1850—Criticism and interpretation. 3. Coleridge, Samuel
Taylor, 1772-1834—Criticism and interpretation. 4. Keats, John, 1795-
1821—Criticism and interpretation. 5. English poetry—Men authors—History
and criticism. 6. Masculinity (Psychology) in literature. 7. Power (Social
sciences) in literature. 8. Sex (Psychology) in literature. 9. Romanticism—
Great Britain. I. Title.
PR590.W32   1996
821'.7093538—dc20   95-43843

The University Press of Florida is the scholarly publishing agency for the State
University System of Florida, comprised of Florida A & M University, Florida
Atlantic University, Florida International University, Florida State University,
University of Central Florida, University of Florida, University of North
Florida, University of South Florida, and University of West Florida.

University Press of Florida
15 Northwest 15th Street
Gainesville, FL 32611

For Joanna Foster
"Like music on the waters
Is thy sweet voice to me"

Contents

Acknowledgments

I have incurred many debts during the research and writing of this book. I am particularly grateful to the graduate students in my seminar on romanticism and gender several years ago, where many of the ideas in this study were first systematically explored; Rawda Awwad and Brad Hollingshead were especially helpful with their close reading of texts, intellectual curiosity, and sharp, focused questions about history and gender. Many colleagues have also listened patiently as I tried in endless conversations to formulate and articulate clearly my ideas about the connections between romanticism and sadism; I am pleased to acknowledge a debt of gratitude to Linda Kinnahan, Brent Peterson, Magali Michael, Tony Rosso, Terry Hoagwood, Jay Keenan, and Sam Tindall. Walda Metcalf of the University Press of Florida has provided much needed encouragement and guidance, exhibiting both patience and a firm sense of direction as the manuscript passed through several readers and revisions. William D. Brewer and Greg Kucich read the manuscript in its entirety and offered excellent suggestions for revision; I am grateful to them for their excellent suggestions for revision. I also wish to thank two anonymous readers who offered detailed and challenging responses to the manuscript. I also wish to express my heartfelt gratitude to Kathy Grossman, whose steadiness, integrity, and kindness during very difficult times gave me strength to continue work on this project. My greatest debt is to Joanna Foster, to whom this study is dedicated.

An outstanding recent article by Robert N. Essick, "Gender, Transgression, and the Two Wordsworths in 'Tintern Abbey,'" appeared too late for consideration in this study (*Texas Studies in Literature and*

Language 36 [1994]: 291–305). Essick's essay is one of the most original and intelligent investigations of gender in *Tintern Abbey* to appear, and I call attention to it here because it treats (from a slightly different angle) many of the issues presented in my discussion of Wordsworth's poem.

A shorter version of the Keats chapter was published previously as "History, Self, and Gender in *Ode to Psyche*," in Nicholas Roe, ed., *Keats and History*, 88–106, and I am grateful to Cambridge University Press for permission to reprint it here.

Introduction

In the current historical reassessment of romanticism, gender has rightly become a major area of scholarly and critical focus. The work on gender has unfolded in at least four directions. A major effort is now under way (led by Stuart Curran) to recover the work of women poets who wrote during the romantic period and who have been forgotten by literary history. Several critics, especially Marlon Ross and Anne Mellor, have begun to identify and investigate a tradition of women's writing that developed against the canonical (masculinist) literature of the period. Still other critics, such as Barbara Schapiro and Laurie Langbauer, have investigated the psychological and cultural dimensions of the feminine during the romantic period, with particular attention to mothering. Finally, as seen in the work of Ross and Alan Richardson, some critics have begun to examine the way (male) romantic literature appropriates, or colonizes, things feminine.[1] Perhaps the most salutary effect of these critical and scholarly efforts to foreground the fact, place, and function of gender in the romantic imagination is that they have begun to raise important questions concerning some of romanticism's most closely held assumptions about the nature and character of human experience and to provide a means for critically questioning those assumptions. In doing so, moreover, feminist criticism has brought new intellectual energy to the study of romanticism, focusing certain nuances of romantic expression and meaning and opening up romantic texts and culture to new levels of understanding.

One important question that has begun to press to the surface of critical discussion in the feminist investigation of romanticism is whether the romantic imagination is *essentially* masculinist—that is, whether romantic expression necessitates the exclusion or suppression of feminine identity—and, if so, whether its masculinist center devastates the romantic visionary project, including its expressed utopian desire for a transformed and redeemed world. If the controlling feature of romanticism is a masculine identity that appropriates and subordinates femininity, then feminists must question whether romanticism's utopian desire for a transformed world can in any respect be endorsed by feminism, whose goal is gender equality. Put slightly differently, and perhaps reductively, if the romantic imagination is essentially masculinist, then, despite its utopian character, it is an obstacle to human liberation and must be rejected.

To cast the issue in such strong terms suggests what ultimately is at stake in the feminist critique of romanticism. To place gender at the center of critical discussion not only forces a fundamental reassessment of romantic utopian thought or of literary history; it also opens the way for a broader reconsideration of a complex range of historical issues. In reassessing romantic visionary idealism in the light of gender stratification, feminism in effect addresses questions about the political dynamics of gender in history, about the character of utopian thought, and therefore about the historical grounds for a goal-oriented feminist politics seeking to transform the present. The feminist critique of visionary romanticism, in other words, is not simply a study of literature and the past but also a statement about the present and future.

This book contributes to the debate over romanticism and gender by examining the cultural logic of visionary romanticism. The aim is to identify certain historical and social conditions that both delimit and energize canonical romantic poems and thereby to expose masculinist tendencies within romanticism while at the same time—by reading romanticism from a social historical, rather than literary historical, perspective—preserving some portions of romantic idealism. This objective at times entails a strong and even severe reading of romantic poems in an effort to implicate them as thoroughly as possible in the cultural logic of their age. But the strategy is not only deconstructive, and, as I say, the conclusion is not dismissive; rather my effort is to place romanticism in its historical and ideological complexity in the belief that only in this way can romantic utopian desire be fully understood, recuperated, and put in the service of a historicist and feminist project.

It may be worth recalling here a comment made by Irene Tayler a few years ago about another book-length feminist study of romanticism. In reviewing the book for the *Keats-Shelley Journal,* Tayler laments its harsh language (the book claims that male romantic writers "cannibalize" the feminine), commenting that such language "illustrates our profession's habit of privileging literary violence of poetic figuring over that of physical reality."[2] Although this statement is part of a book review rather than a substantive critical study, it nevertheless provides an important caveat to feminist criticism because it emphasizes how easy it is to lose sight of a larger complexity—and decency—that may reside in poems written by men and that poetic expression is not the same thing as physical assault. At the same time, however, physical violence often is part of a cultural logic that manifests itself in many ways—including poetry—and it is important to trace that logic across the full range of social and cultural life in an effort to loosen its grip. The difficult challenge is to recognize, as Tayler does, forms of inequality—or even violence—when they appear in poetry, while at the same time not losing sight of larger and deeper currents of a more benevolent human desire that may characterize poetic expression.

I call these issues to mind here because I am aware that my own argument is in many respects guilty of the charges that Tayler properly brings against the feminist study described in her review—and because I think that Tayler is right that romantic poetry cannot be reduced to matters of violence or matters of masculine oppression. But, again, while my investigation of gender offers a strong reading of the logic of violence within romanticism, my objective is intended to be constructive and recuperative. The singular attention to gender stratification, gender violence, and gender anxiety in the present study is meant not to devastate the project of romantic visionary idealism but rather to insist that romanticism be understood and explained as history rather than consumed as nostalgia.

Because I call upon history as the authority for my argument, I want now to offer a few schematic generalizations about romanticism and history that may help to contextualize, or ground, the critique that I offer of specific romantic writers and poems.

Romanticism is characterized most profoundly by its relation to the transition, in Britain, from feudalism to capitalism. This claim has been argued persuasively by Robert Sayre and Michael Lowy, who define and defend romanticism as utopian desire for precapitalist values; that desire, they argue, while directed to the past, can be used as the basis for a critique of the quantifying and alienating authority of capitalism. For Sayre and Lowy, romanticism constitutes a challenge to, and points a way out of, capitalism's reduction of human life to so many economic units.[3]

While Sayre and Lowy emphasize in helpful ways the antagonistic relation of romanticism to capitalism, their argument must be modified to resist certain essentialist assumptions that seem to undergird it. The presentation of their claim that romanticism is best understood as a cultural response to the historical triumph of industrial capitalism in the late eighteenth and early nineteenth centuries is remarkably erudite and persuasive; but it does not adequately consider the complicated ways that British romanticism, even in its most utopian moments, remains deeply entangled within the social and cultural conditions of both feudalism and capitalism. The attachment of romanticism to feudal and aristocratic subject matter is too fond to be seen only as a rejection of capitalist values; that attachment constitutes as well a historical residue that marks the continuing hold of an aristocratic worldview on at least a portion of the romantic imagination. At the time romanticism emerges, alongside industrial capitalism, feudalism has not yet entirely let go its hold on the cultural imagination, a fact that forces a more careful consideration than Sayre and Lowy have provided of the dialectical warfare between the residual cultural claims of feudalism, the emergent economic-cultural demands of capitalism, and the place of romanticism within this turbulent situation.

Moreover, the romantic rejection of capitalism—seen in British literature in the retreat into nature, the creation of beautiful idealisms unmolested by urban and economic pressure, and the scathing portrayals, especially by Blake and Shelley, of England's dark satanic mills—cannot be satisfactorily explained only as an escape from capitalism. In important ways, the romantic rejection of capitalism is at the same time an embrace—and reflection—of some of its most fundamental values: the rejection of a sordid world, the embrace of subjectivity, the attention to the particular as opposed to the structural, the retreat into private pleasures afforded by nature—these and more are powerful signs of the triumph of capitalism in its maneuver to organize and secure its own authority by fragmenting human life into privatized, or atomized, units. To see romantic subjectivity and utopian vision only, or primarily, as a virtue is to forget how entirely necessary subjectivity and utopia were to the economic and cultural operations of an emergent industrial capitalist state.[4]

If romanticism emerges as a response to capitalism, then, that response is governed in important ways by capitalism itself, and a historical investigation of romanticism must consider how its liberating and hopeful components stand in relation to the world that it would transcend, escape, or transform.

The problematic relation of romanticism to the economic and cultural complexities associated with the transition from feudalism to capitalism must be understood alongside the relation of romanticism to the failure of the Enlightenment project to create a bourgeois public sphere.[5] Just as romanticism cannot be read solely as a rejection or embrace of capitalism and its culture, neither can it be read solely as a rejection of the Enlightenment, though there often has been a tendency to do so. While romanticism (as Blake's work explicitly demonstrates) certainly refuses the more authoritarian and totalizing impulses of Enlightenment reason as well as the Enlightenment construction of a despiritualized nature and the Enlightenment commitment to public conduct and exchange, it does not overleap Enlightenment thought in its desire to reenchant nature or in its nostalgic turn to feudal and aristocratic ideals. For all its disruptive energies, romanticism remains ideologically committed to certain categories constituent of the Enlightenment: reason is tamed but preserved; nature remains prominent, though in reenchanted form; progress is valued, though lifted to spiritual and idealized levels. The relation of romantic and Enlightenment thought is one not only of discontinuity but also of continuity; it is impossible to speak of romantic texts and ideas without considering the way that the intellectual and cultural projects that preceded romanticism continue to exercise their shaping authority even after they have been rejected or transformed.[6]

My third and final general claim involves the problematic nature and status of gender in the romantic imagination. As I have suggested, the challenge facing the historical-feminist reassessment of romanticism not only requires the recovery of works by women, tracking instances of the romantic mother, and showing how the feminine is often colonized in romantic texts; ultimately critical investigation must consider as well the romantic construction of gender *in relation to* the changing structures of historical, social, and cultural authority during the romantic period. To what extent, for example, does romanticism's entanglement in the turbulent conditions of both feudalism and capitalism, or its involvement with the declining energy of the Enlightenment project, shape the romantic understanding and portrayal of gender? Is the commonly recognized idealization of the feminine in romantic texts always a sign of patriarchal authority over the feminine, or might it also

signify that the feminine had come to be charged with a unique historical energy? Is the frequent demonization of the feminine, seen most
often, but not only, in gothic texts, always a sign of romantic contempt
for women, or might it signify as well a disruptive energy that challenges and threatens to subvert prevailing (masculine) orders of authority? Further, are these formulations of the feminine the product of men's
imagination only, or are they mediated in important ways by economic
and cultural claims being staked out by the various declining and
emergent structures of social authority during the period? If the latter,
then how do we best read the mediations of gender, both feminine and
masculine?

Such questions as these, along with many related questions, can be
considered most usefully when gender is cast in its strongest possible
form and then set in relation to other prominent, or constitutive,
features of romanticism. I am speaking of the problematic and urgent
significance of sadeian logic in the romantic imagination. The feminist
critique of gender in the romantic imagination turns very largely on the
question of whether sadism, which emerged historically alongside romanticism, is a deviation from romantic desire—the dark other side of
romanticism—or a necessary and constitutive dimension of romanticism.[7] If it is a deviation, a phenomenon of such perversity and extremity that it can have no bearing on the ordinary operations of the
romantic formulation of gender, then it is automatically contained: it
can be ignored, and the romantic view of gender can be explained on
the terms set by romanticism itself. But if sadeian logic is seen to be
historically linked to romanticism, then feminist critical labor becomes
immensely complex, for it must establish the nature of that link; theorize the relations between sadism and the transformation of eighteenth-
and nineteenth-century society and culture, particularly the relations
between sadism and capitalism; and determine whether, or to what
extent, the cultural presence of sadeian thought helps to condition the
relations between romanticism and capitalism and contaminates romantic utopian hope. The presence of sadeian logic as a cultural authority or pressure, in short, threatens to change fundamentally the historical explanation of romanticism and romantic texts.[8]

These three admittedly nonparallel categories of society, philosophy,
and sexuality seem to me to be crucial in the attempt to locate and
explain, in historical terms, the romantic imagination and romantic
textuality. The structural transformation of British society from feudal-

ism to capitalism, an Enlightenment project that ideologically serves this transformation and then partly collapses and the sudden reality of sadeian logic as a cultural problematic converge in the late eighteenth century, not as a coherent worldview but as conflicting forces that both energize and delimit cultural consciousness and that arise and sink within textual practice in compelling, complex ways. While the relations among these categories may never be thoroughly or definitively mapped, as they unfold at various levels of historical development, with varying degrees of intensity, and often appear only in the extreme margins of romantic texts, their urgent significance—as historically related energies and enabling textual currents—to the study of romanticism is nevertheless certain and bears systematic investigation.

In the following chapters, several poems by Wordsworth, Coleridge, and Keats will serve as a test case for working through, in a general fashion, some of these issues and concerns. Particularly, I want to situate the poems within a historical frame that acknowledges the tensions between feudalism and capitalism—not tensions that existed only at the moment of the 1790s but that define the large structural transformation of British society and culture from the sixteenth to the nineteenth century[9]—in an effort to consider the impact of those tensions on certain ideological problems connected to romantic thought; to examine the relevance of these to the romantic understanding of gender; and to question how these various matters bear on the cultural life of poetic expression. This critical endeavor, again, calls romanticism to historical account on the issue of gender while at the same time suggesting that the frequent questionable romantic portrayals of gender contain as well their dialectical opposite, which might be useful in the feminist effort to construct a liberating and historically credible vision of gender.

Chapter One

Romanticism, Sadism, and
the Question of Critical Method

1.

It has been more than sixty years since Mario Praz published the first edition of his controversial study of the relations between romanticism and sadism. Ranging across the literatures of several nations, across many genres, and across a wide literary historical span (from Richardson's *Clarissa* [1747–48] to Isidore Ducasse's *Chants de Maldoror* [1868]), Praz documents the many instances and permutations of the theme of the persecuted maiden in the eighteenth and nineteenth centuries.[1] While he acknowledges that literary portrayals of violence against women are "as old as the world," he maintains that, after a period of relative quiet in literary history, sexual violence appeared with renewed force and significance in the imagination of the eighteenth century, culminated in the violent writings of Sade, and took its place as a common theme in a diverse body of subsequent literature in the nineteenth century.[2] It was Praz's great contribution to articulate the central importance of this literary development to the historical understanding and definition of romanticism and to confirm the frequency with which sexual violence appears in romantic literature, culture, and psychology.

Praz's immense labors in *The Romantic Agony* are important to romantic scholarship not only because they bring to light issues and themes that long had been passed over without serious critical commentary but also because they suggest many areas where further scholarly work might (and should) be carried out. Extensive archival research is needed to determine with greater precision how pervasive sexually

1

explicit and sadistic literature was during the period and to what extent this literature influenced other kinds of literary production.[3] Critical speculation about the origins of sexual violence in English literature—and, more specifically, about how the literary representations of sexual violence in the seventeenth century differ from those in the nineteenth—could be helpfully refined beyond the broad-brush presentation by Praz. Most importantly, a theory of the cultural connections between gender relations (or patriarchal power relations) and romantic literature and culture, hinted at but never fully developed in the *Romantic Agony*, ought to be elaborated so that a fuller and more precise understanding of the social-historical dimensions of romanticism can be advanced. That very little of this work has been undertaken over the past sixty years is not altogether surprising,[4] as Praz's book generated considerable controversy in its day (commented upon by Praz in the preface to the second edition of his work), and this controversy seems to have been taken as a warning by subsequent scholars that the connections between romanticism and sexual violence constitute a treacherous cultural-intellectual territory better left alone.[5] The result is that the work begun by Praz has advanced very little, and in fact critical interest in the relations between romanticism (particularly canonical romantic texts) and sexual violence has receded into virtual obscurity.

Even the recent proliferation of historical and feminist investigations of romanticism has barely begun to investigate the kinds of cultural territory brought into view by Praz's work.[6] One consequence of the failure of scholars to pursue many of the vital leads provided by Praz is that some of the most important intellectual and critical issues bearing on the historical study of romanticism and gender remain untheorized. For example, the precise relationship between the sexual violence, or sexual oppression, about which Praz writes and the visionary hope found in the idealizing romantic imagination has yet to be fully explored, despite the fact that the romantic imagination is caught up in quite gender-specific ways with questions of power and violence. Nor have critics adequately examined, from a historical perspective, important related questions about how and why gender relations in romantic literature take the form they do or about how those relations, often hidden in the deep structure of texts, govern the surface structure of romantic texts. Until these and similar issues have been thoroughly investigated and theorized, historicist and feminist critics of romantic literature cannot point a satisfactory direction out of the oppressive patriarchal networks of power that they rightly have shown are registered in many romantic texts. But carrying out such an investigation, as Praz learned, carries risks because it entails an argument that seems calculated to debilitate the romantic visionary project.

In fact, the long tradition of romantic historical criticism—as several excellent historicist studies over the past ten years have shown—has for the most part steadfastly refused to examine too closely its own indebtedness to romantic expressions and assumptions about gender, choosing too often to take its intellectual cue not from, say, its own independently derived critical assumptions or objectives but rather from the romantic perspective that it sets out to examine. This curious way of approaching the vexed cultural terrain of romanticism and gender (which would seem to assume that a romantic explanation of romantic issues commands special authority) is perhaps most readily apparent in the tendency of criticism to situate its analysis almost entirely at the level of plot and theme while leaving the empowering networks of social relations behind them unexamined: what romantic literature presents as thematically important, in other words, is too often accepted as the necessary context of critical investigation rather than considered as a symptom, sign, or visible manifestation of deeper and more far-reaching historical currents that may carry within them structures of value and belief that contradict romantic cultural expression.[7]

The many investigations, for example, of the romantic sublime and romantic gothic have said much about the so-called dark side of romanticism—that is, about the romantic habit of thematizing the loneliness, dread, and even violence of human experience that stand counter to predominant romantic assumptions about ideal beauty and human possibility—but have done little to clarify the cultural assumptions about the relations of gender lying behind the dark and brooding themes of gothic or to explain why and how these themes are so often inextricably connected to the romantic desire for the beautiful.[8] The same may be said of innumerable plot-level details in the gothic and nongothic literature of the period. The brutal murder of Elizabeth Lavenza in *Frankenstein*, the rape of Antonia and murder of Elvira in Matthew Lewis's *The Monk*, the rape of Beatrice Cenci in Shelley's brutal drama, the attempted belittlement of Maria Velez in Coleridge's *Osorio*, the murder of Floribel in Beddoes's *The Brides' Tragedy*, the oppression of Parisina in Byron's Eastern Tale, the marginalization of Dorothy in *Tintern Abbey*, the sexual thrill inextricably bound to Christabel's lonely fate, the violent struggles between masculine specters and feminine emanations in the work of Blake, the sexual violation of Madeline in *The Eve of St. Agnes*—these and many more plot-level details are readily seen as examples of sexual violence but are usually accepted, finally, on the terms set down by romantic cultural expression itself as evidence of certain dark, disturbing, and yet unavoidable facts of human experience that the romantic imagination would seek to transcend or as examples of a troubled individual psychology whose tendencies are apparently undetermined and unmediated by social reality. They are seldom treated as necessary or constituent features of a historically generated romantic vision of human life and possibility, integrally connected by means of a cultural logic to the many noble romantic expressions of desire for ideal beauty and truth.[9]

2.

One way of directing literary criticism past such (in my view) narrowly constrained perspectives on romanticism and gender is by aligning it with the assumptions and strategies of historical materialism. A historical materialist criticism offers not only the most comprehensive and persuasive methodology for investigating social relations (including gender) and historical logic (including patriarchy) but also tremendous explanatory authority in analyzing the details of individual literary texts. Moreover, while it recognizes the socially generated contradictions inherent in literary texts, at the same time its strategies are ultimately constructive rather than deconstructive. Indeed, a historical materialist methodology can open the way to a positive radical reassessment of literature and its interpretation not because it grounds critical practice in what texts cannot say, and not because it sets itself antagonistically against other critical strategies, but rather because it energetically enlists texts—literary and critical—in its effort to discover and explain an inner historical logic of human activity, including such imaginative and intellectual activity as poetry and criticism.

One of the interests of historical materialism that distinguishes it most emphatically from some of the narrower academic versions of poststructuralism is its insistence upon a single (nontextual) human activity, or history, within which all questions of meaning and language—and textuality—must necessarily be framed, even if their representation must rely on a textual strategy. This perspective rejects the positivist desire to find "truth" in the correspondences between representation and referent as well as the Hegelian desire to explain history in terms of a transhistorical Absolute, resting its credibility, rather, upon the clear assumption that all knowledge, value, and meaning are always dialectically caught up with and mediated by human need and human practice. A thoroughly secular perspective, insofar as it does not begin from a notion of spiritual essence, it locates its conceptual tools and its logic—and finds its critical path—in what people do; while people may (or may not) be constituted as subjects along various discursive paths (as some versions of poststructuralism might argue), it is they themselves who produce that path and shape the conditions of its authority, even as they themselves are shaped by material circumstance.

What this means for literary criticism is, among other things, that whether critical activity is formalist, biographical, or psychological in nature, it is subject to the material conditions under which it is carried out. While a poststructuralist criticism, for instance, might wish to see texts solely in terms of their formal, discursive, and linguistic properties, it is nevertheless forced to register certain historical energies that enliven these properties: in the last instance, one might say, formal and language-based analyses are also historical analyses. As Fredric Jameson puts it, "all apparently formal statements about a work bear within them a concealed historical dimension of which the critic is not often aware."[10] A simple and (to me) obvious idea, to be sure, this position nonetheless has the intellectual advantage of allowing the critic to draw analytical distinctions without making category mistakes: language and referent, and form and content, must be analytically distinguished for the purposes of investigation and explanation, but this does not mean that they are entirely distinct and autonomous categories; they are, rather, categories set in dialectical relation to one another within the historical frame of human activity.[11] While the newer strategies of poststructuralism—and the older strategies of formal analysis—are certainly right to draw critical attention to the conflict, difference, and discontinuity that characterize the various textual representations of human activity, they are wrong, or limited, when they fail to consider the historical commonalities upon which these textual representations are necessarily grounded.

To insist upon the determining authority of a single historical presence is to understand that Keats, for instance, is both an individual from the past *and* a cultural idea constructed through various forms of critical and linguistic practice over time; that history includes the events and ideas associated with Keats's own day, the narrative representation of those events and ideas, *and* the situation from which a literary critic approaches Keats; that the meaning of Keats's poetry derives from the material conditions under which it was produced *and* from the ways in which that poetry is appropriated, described, and used by individuals and cultures over time.[12] Past and present; form and content; language and its referents; the world, the text, and the critic—these participate in a single, dialectical, process of discovering and producing knowledge, meaning, and value, a process whose significance lies partly in the fact that it provides information about, and provides a means for changing, the present by telling about the lived relation of the past to the present. Again to cite Jameson on historical materialism: "For a Marxist historicism . . . the presupposition is that none of . . . [the] forms of the past are of antiquarian interest alone, and that their actuality for us may be demonstrated—indeed, can only be demonstrated—by an analysis that juxtaposes the limits and the potentialities of our own socioeconomic moment with those realized or imposed by the systems of the past, in short, by other *modes of production.*"[13]

To place a slightly different emphasis on Jameson's point, one might say that historical materialism would see Keats's poems as so many verbal artifacts whose significance arises from their *relation to* conditions that exist apart from, and yet are necessary to and inscribed in, their textuality. Such a view would not deny the integrity of the textual and literary qualities of Keats's poetry but would argue rather that those qualities can be conceptualized, explained, and *valued* only in terms of what are generally regarded to be extratextual and extraliterary considerations. Even if those considerations can be accessed only textually, through scholarly and critical language, they are nonetheless antecedent to textuality, and they constitute the necessary assumptions upon which interpretative investigation depends.

The sort of position I am describing here is meant to be sufficiently flexible to encourage not only recent, poststructuralist, forms of criticism that self-reflexively foreground the critical act itself and the complex operations of language but also traditional sorts of historical research into the sources and contexts of romantic cultural expression. But it would do so while at the same time insisting that neither the newer critical practice nor the older historical research is ideologically neutral, for, as I have suggested, its most basic assumption is that a poetic text to which is attached the name of Keats or Wordsworth or Byron can never be entirely separated (formally or interpretatively) from various social and historical pressures that determine its shape as well as the significance of its investigation. What this means, of course, is that for historical materialism the acts of knowing and explaining writers and their poetry are always, on some level, political acts insofar as they participate in a cultural process of discovering, producing, shaping, and disseminating human value, meaning, and knowledge. The important critical work of Earl Wasserman on Shelley, no less than the brilliant and combative recent work of Marjorie Levinson on Keats, is engaged not simply in transmitting a stable body of knowledge but also in producing a knowledge that plays its small part in shaping the meaning and direction of the culture of which Keats and Shelley studies are a part.[14]

3.

Historical materialism offers a powerful means of explaining the underlying structural determinants and dimensions of sexual power in romantic literature. Part of its authority derives from the fact that it does not initiate analysis from within the context of issues that romantic literature has thematized, for it recognizes that this would necessarily entrap critique in the terms established by romanticism itself. Rather, materialist analysis begins from within historically defined networks of power that determine the particular literary and cultural contours of romanticism and that only gradually become thematized, at times as the beautiful and, at other times, as the sublime. This abandonment of literary plot and theme as the starting points of criticism brackets out most conventional literary historical definitions of romanticism as well, thereby creating the possibility of an analysis grounded in two distinctly different and apparently alien sets of intellectual and historical concern that are usually elided by the romantic imagination but that nonetheless have determining significance for romanticism: assumptions—upon which the themes of sadism are constructed—about violence as a constituent feature of human nature, ineluctably bound to the drive for pleasure; and the structural transformation of the British class system that was accelerated during the romantic period.

While there is no fully elaborated theoretical model to enable a discussion of romanticism in the precise terms that I am here proposing, two important works may be taken as guides in the effort to construct such a model. Angela Carter's controversial theories of the sadeian text, in *The Sadeian Woman,* and Robert Sayre and Michael Lowy's erudite discussion of romanticism as a historical phenomenon, in "Figures of Romantic Anticapitalism," consider widely divergent aspects of art and culture during the late eighteenth and early nineteenth centuries. In isolation from one another, their discussions are only minimally useful in the investigation of romanticism and sexual violence; but when their various objects of investigation and conceptual procedures are brought together, they can provide the basis for a comprehensive and compelling analysis of the subject—an analysis that can be used to challenge and redirect conventional understanding of romanticism by exposing the forms of violence attached to romantic visionary idealism while at the same time keeping alive the positive *historical* power of romantic desire.

Before sketching the content of these two works, I want to describe explicitly the critical position that I am attempting to construct from a synthesis of the Carter and Sayre-Lowy arguments. My concern is not so much with the particular narratives of Sade or with the expressions of hope or despair—or sexual violence—in individual romantic texts; it is, rather, with the historical and cultural logic that came to maturation in the late eighteenth and early nineteenth centuries with the final political, economic, and ideological victories of the bourgeoisie and that, I believe, helps to shape in fundamental ways sadeian and romantic cultural expression. That logic, put simply, is held in place by the common assumption that human identity necessarily arises from one person's absolute domination of another. That logic further assumes that pleasure, hope, and human fullness depend upon an entirely discrete individual identity and, therefore, upon the domination, or exclusion, of other identities, which might threaten autonomy. Under the authority of such a logic, even the most sincere (romantic) expressions of human value are implicated in unequal relations of power. The domination that stands at the center of what may properly be called sadeian logic may be expressed in terms of physical violence, as it often is in the writings of Sade, or (say) Matthew Lewis; or it may be expressed ideologically as the idealization of one person (usually a woman) by another (usually a man), as it often is in the poetry of Shelley. But in either case women are rendered powerless, or dependent, and the identity expressed in the sadeian or romantic text is masculine.[15]

While these critical assumptions will be specified and argued in subsequent chapters, I state them directly here because I want to be clear that I am not concerned with finding parallels between narrative episodes in Sade's *Justine,* for instance, and the plot-level details of any particular romantic poem. My concern, rather, as I have suggested, is with the deep structures of authority and belief that underlie and help to shape plot and theme, and particularly with the operations of those structures with respect to gender relations. At this level of investigation it becomes possible to glimpse the historical currents that carry within them such apparently contradictory cultural expressions as romanticism and sadism and therefore to explain the social relations of gender that inform both the hope and dread, fear and desire, that characterize those relations in European culture during the late eighteenth and early nineteenth centuries. A historicist explanation along these lines also forces critics and scholars today to reconsider the ideological burdens carried by romantic utopian thought and—what follows from this—to consider whether those burdens vitiate the many romantic expressions of hope for justice, equality, and human emancipation.

4.

The relations between sadism and class struggle are brilliantly examined in Carter's *The Sadeian Woman*, which elaborates the historical dimensions of these issues during the romantic period without specific consideration of how they shape romantic literature and imagination. Carter's argument provides one of the crucial missing links to recent historical and feminist readings of romanticism. Both critical and constructive in nature, it proceeds along methodological lines that can enable a historically motivated feminism to expose the patriarchal and oppressive tendencies within romanticism while at the same time providing a basis for exploring how certain transformative political energies within romanticism might be preserved.

The line of Carter's argument rests upon her assumption that sexual violence and class struggle were integrally connected in the late eighteenth century and, more specifically, that the sexual violence described in the writings of the aristocratic Sade lays bare the class violence accompanying the transition from feudalism to capitalism in the 1790s. Without reducing sexual issues entirely to class issues, Carter demonstrates how a new bourgeois world order reconstructs relations of gender to meet its historically specific needs and how, in the works of Sade, this reconstitution is shown to take place while (and by) eliding the historicity of gender. While every act of sexual violence in Sade's works, as in all pornography, appears to be removed entirely from all historical contexts and networks of social exchange, in fact there is a high degree of social and class specificity informing sadistic sexual activity. Sadeian libertines occupy a range of carefully defined class positions; as Carter states, they "are great aristocrats, landowners, bankers, judges, archbishops, popes, and certain women who have become very rich through prostitution, speculation, murder and usury." Sade periodically interrupts their orgies of sex and violence to offer

lengthy "philosphical sermons on the family, on marriage, contracep-
tion, abortion, prostitution, cruelty and love."[16] The particular handling of class in Sade's portrayal of sexual violence makes his pornographic vision synonymous with the violent conflicts of history. And, as
Carter persuasively argues, Sade's repeated denial of this fact in many
philosophical statements on the nature and meaning of sexual violence
is itself inextricably caught in the vexed class and social relations
forming the center of that history.

The class dimension of Sade's pornographic vision is evident everywhere in his work, and, in its sexual representation, it reduces to a
chillingly simple fact: in the world that Sade describes, "women are
commodities,"[17] transformed from humans into objects for the purpose
of purchase and exchange.[18] This point is perhaps confused by the fact
that virtually all of Sade's libertines come from an aristocratic rather
than bourgeois ruling class, thus raising questions about whether their
actions legitimately may be said to reflect class conflict in a market-
driven world. But the decisive factor in a historicist reading of Sade is
not simply the class position that an individual character occupies but
rather the network of class relations—including their ideological authority—that limit and enable a character's thought and actions. Sade's
male aristocratic libertines may seldom be cast (say) as middle class
entrepreneurs, but they nevertheless often reflect an entrepreneurial
mindset as they trade in the flesh of women, a fact that suggests the
decline of aristocratic ideology, the violence, horror, and even desire
accompanying that decline, and the desperate effort of a doomed class
to assert, one last time, its power by drawing upon the energies and
social logic of an emergent (bourgeois) class in pursuing its ends.

In Sade's vision, these class realities are most often cast graphically in
terms of the violent fate of women. Whereas in the orthodox Marxian
formulation, men as workers under capitalism sell their labor power,
thereby placing an exchange value on it, women (as not only Sade but
also Christina Rossetti, in the mid-nineteenth century, seems to have
understood)[19] are required also to sell their bodies or to put their bodies
in circulation in the marketplace for the purpose of male sexual pleasure. This means that human flesh, rather than simply human labor
power, or the products of human labor, is subject to the quantifying
processes of capitalist reification, magically transformed into an object
for circulation and consumption within the social structures and relations of commodity exchange. Sade's Justine resists these demands of
circulation and exchange—which are also the demands of bourgeois

patriarchy—and is accordingly raped, beaten, and in other ways physically and emotionally violated by an economic and class system capable of crushing all resistance. On the other hand, her counterpart and sister, Juliette, readily puts her body in circulation, her personal fortunes and pleasures thereby following clearly the economic course of capitalism.[20] Within this oppressive and exploitative class structure (the world of the market and of the commodity), governed by men, masculine sexual pleasure that is derived from various forms of consumption of the female body becomes the rough equivalent of what Marx calls, in discussing the expropriation of human labor power, surplus value: male orgasm is the profit derived from the sexual exploitation and consumption of women. And, as the Marxian analysis of surplus value shows, behind the process of exploitation and expropriation stand the transformation of human capabilities into inhuman things and, ultimately, the denial to human flesh of all its humanity, until even the very soul and spirit of humanity are consumed by capitalism.

Whether or not Carter is correct in arguing that the works of Sade, in their portrayal of class and sexual relations, can become a friend to the feminist struggle for freedom and equality (Andrea Dworkin argues heatedly, and at times persuasively, that they cannot),[21] she is certainly correct in locating the sadeian vision of human sexuality at the historical moment of the triumph of a bourgeois worldview, in maintaining that bourgeois patriarchy possesses its own historically specific definition of gender, and in sketching the peculiar demands that bourgeois patriarchy places on women; she is right, in other words, in arguing that "flesh comes to us out of history"[22] and in attempting to elaborate a materialist theory of this position. Her analysis is thus potentially useful in the effort to elaborate the interrelations of gender, class, and social structure in the literature of romanticism, a literature produced under the same violent historical logic and at the identical and embracing historical moment that Sade was writing—the moment of the demise of aristocracy and the triumph of the bourgeoisie.

5.

The importance of Carter's analysis for romanticism becomes clear when it is set alongside Sayre and Lowy's "Figures of Romantic Anticapitalism," one of the most ambitious theoretical and historicist considerations of romanticism to appear in the last twenty years. I want, therefore, to sketch briefly the major trajectory of the Sayre-Lowy argument, both stressing its crucial contributions to the historical study of romanticism and (using Carter as a guide) interrogating its more problematic assertions and assumptions. I will follow this sketch with a consideration of how certain of its elements can be helpfully modified by and integrated with Carter's theory of sexual violence in the late eighteenth century to provide the basis for a historical explanation of romanticism and gender.

At the heart of the Sayre-Lowy argument is their persuasive definition of romanticism as a historically specific worldview rather than as a purely literary, or cultural, phenomenon reducible to a definable set of formal features or literary themes or genres. This historical worldview develops within, and is an intellectual and imaginative response to, an emergent and triumphant industrial capitalism, whose relentlessly expanding mechanism seeks to quantify all human relations; to subject an ever widening circle of culture and society to its quantifying power; and, ultimately, to transform people themselves into objects to be used, consumed, and discarded. As a response to industrial capitalism and its a hegemonic bourgeois social order, romanticism is marked by both "contradictions" and an "essential unity."[23] That is, its unifying principle is its rejection of the values of capitalism in favor of precapitalist values, a fact that would seem to place romanticism directly at odds with the sadeian logic described by Carter. As Sayre and Lowy put it: "The romantic soul longs ardently to return home, and it is precisely the *nostalgia* for what has been lost that is at the center of the romantic anti-capitalist vision."[24] At the same time, the form that the romantic rejection of capitalist values takes is highly variable, manifesting itself sometimes as reactionary and sometimes as revolutionary.

Sayre and Lowy provide a typology of these romantic responses to capitalism, sketching the features that distinguish each response from the other while at the same time linking them through their common opposition to an industrial capitalist world order. Among the forms of revolutionary romanticism, Sayre and Lowy name Jacobin-democratic romanticism, "which adopts a critical stance toward both feudalism and the new aristocracy of wealth"; populist romanticism, "which opposes industrial capitalism as monarchy and serfdom"; Utopian-humanist socialism, which "designate[s] those socialist currents and thinkers who aspire to a collectivist [postcapitalist] utopia, but who do not see the industrial proletariat as the historical agent of this project"; libertarian romanticism, "which draws on the pre-capitalist, collectivist traditions of peasants, artisans, and skilled workers in their revolutionary struggle against capitalism"; and Marxist romanticism, which uses "nostalgia for a precapitalist *Gemeinschaft* . . . both as a motivating force for the critique of industrial capitalism and as a crucial element in the socialist utopia of the future."[25] At the other pole of the historical dialectic are less revolutionary and occasionally even reactionary forms of romanticism, which nevertheless are unified in their rejection of capitalist values: restitutionist romanticism, which is defined by its "desire to restore or recreate . . . a [precapitalist] past state in the present";[26] conservative romanticism, which is defined as the effort to "legitimate the established order by interpreting it as a 'natural result of historical evolution'";[27] fascist romanticism, which blends "the rejection of capitalism . . . with a violent condemnation of parliamentary democracy as well as of Communism," is anti-Semitic, glorifies "the irrational in its pure form," and suppresses "the individualistic pole of romanticism" to an overriding commitment to a movement or state;[28] resigned romanticism, which grudgingly accepts capitalism but longs for a precapitalist world nonetheless; and liberal romanticism, which criticizes the modern bourgeois world without "draw[ing] the radical conclusions following from this criticism, and is content simply to call for reforms rather than for more fundamental change."[29]

One central and controversial component of Sayre and Lowy's thesis is their contention that romanticism is not an example of bourgeois ideology but rather, at its most basic level, a rejection of that ideology. Even the conservative and reactionary elements of romanticism are most properly defined against the historical current of the bourgeois social order. When specific romantic writers come from bourgeois origins, too, Sayre and Lowy argue, and produce the various subjectivist expressions of alienation that have come to be readily associated, often negatively by socialist critics, with bourgeois self-absorption, their portrayals of loneliness, loss, and dread are nevertheless fundamentally anticapitalist because "the central characteristic of capitalism is that its functioning is entirely determined by *quantitative* values: exchange value, price, profit. There is a fundamental opposition, then, between these two worlds [that is, a world of qualitative values that romanticism desires and a world of quantitative values that capitalism demands], an opposition that creates contradictions and conflicts."[30] While capitalism would control every dimension of social and cultural life, romanticism, in all of its forms, rejects that control, defining itself as a desire for, or vision of, a world free of capitalism's reductive and quantifying social relations.

6.

While Sayre and Lowy's argument is intellectually compelling in every respect, its power, integrity, and persuasion making it a central reference for any serious attempt to rethink the historical determinations of romantic literature and culture, it is also incomplete, and perhaps dangerously so. For in failing to provide a frame of reference for understanding and explaining the historical dimensions of gender, it appears to advance a largely masculinist vision of historical change, political intervention, and romantic, utopian possibility that differs little from more traditional old historicist and liberal humanist explanations of history, culture, and society. Worse, it appears to preclude the possibility of a historically viable feminist critique of romanticism, thus eliding at least one area where bourgeois values may determine the shape of the romantic utopian vision.

Angela Carter's materialist explanation of sadism can help to overcome this clear deficiency in the Sayre-Lowy argument. By using her argument as a feminist and materialist starting point, it becomes possible to expose the hidden essentialist assumptions of the Sayre-Lowy argument and thereby to transform it from an account of romanticism's response to industrial capitalism into a more credible historical materialist account of the relation of gender to romanticism *within* the historical context of an emergent industrial capitalism and bourgeois worldview. One risk in using Carter's argument as a basis for modifying Sayre and Lowy's account is that it may seem to deny entirely the utopian center of romantic expression, thus denying the politically progressive potential that is unique to romanticism and that is defended by Sayre and Lowy. Nevertheless, Carter's work is an appropriate guide to a feminist critique of Sayre and Lowy, and for several reasons. First, Carter and Sayre and Lowy share a materialist view of history, which means that their explanations of different subjects taken from a single historical period are shaped by common intellectual assumptions and methodological strategies. Second, the extremity of Carter's argument brings utopianism—which in the Sayre-Lowy argument may seem to be immune to historical reality—back into the firm grasp of historical necessity, serving as a persuasive reminder that if utopian thought is to be politically viable, it must recognize at every moment the ineluctable reality of history. Third, Carter's vision of the social and historical conditions of violent sexuality forces into critical view certain fundamental relations of gender that the romantic hope defended by Sayre and Lowy does not recognize; the credibility of romantic utopianism depends largely upon whether it can account for and accommodate these culturally pervasive relations that occupy the identical historical moment of romanticism. Finally, and perhaps most importantly, Carter shares with Sayre and Lowy a political vision of the possibility of creating human freedom and justice, even within a world that seems to be controlled entirely by violence, oppression, and the quantification of human experience, and thus her particular focus on gender can sharpen and enliven Sayre and Lowy's account of romantic desire.

The labor of modifying the historical account of romanticism by interposing the disruptive and unsettling theory of Carter is difficult because, at least at the level of conceptual categories, what is required is that the relations between several seemingly incongruous assumptions, embedded in the theories of both Carter and Sayre and Lowy, be disentangled and explained. First, the ugly facts of sexual violence and the commodification of women that Carter associates with a bourgeois world order must be persuasively established as a necessary frame of reference for the romantic imagination as well. Second, assuming that the argument about sexual violence can be made, an even more difficult problem arises: if the cultural assumptions and gender relations behind sadism are in fact intertwined with both romantic and bourgeois structures of authority, then, as I have just suggested, the utopian core of Sayre and Lowy's argument (that is, that romanticism is, in its most irreducible definition, a rejection of the bourgeois quantification and commodification of human experience) must be examined to determine whether it elides and, at least tacitly, endorses the sexual stratification and violence that Carter finds to be powerfully present in the cultural imagination of the late eighteenth century. Under the pressure of Carter's argument, in other words, romantic utopian thought must be reconceptualized and historically resituated if it is to remain viable, from a feminist point of view, as an imaginative force of liberating social transformation.

These complex issues can be addressed initially by stating as precisely as possible the particular intellectual and conceptual relations between Carter's theory of sadism and Sayre and Lowy's theory of romanticism and the difficulties inherent in those relations.

If it is accepted at face value that the essence of romanticism is its rejection of a bourgeois world order (as Sayre and Lowy assert), then one must conclude that Carter's argument about sexuality and sexual violence as products of commodity culture during the late eighteenth and early nineteenth centuries describes something *essentially* unromantic. If her subject matter belongs to a category entirely outside romanticism, however, then it is impossible to explain the presence and significance of the portrayals of violent and oppressive sexual relations in avowedly romantic texts (*The Monk, The Cenci, Frankenstein, The Eve of St. Agnes, The Brides' Tragedy, Christabel,* and so on). To preserve the integrity of the Sayre-Lowy thesis, it seems, it would be necessary to say that every instance of bourgeois patriarchy within a romantic poem is an unromantic detail. But if this is so, does it not mean that the study of *romantic* literature focuses always and only on issues apart from bourgeois patriarchy? Does it not mean, in other words, that the study of romanticism must remain silent about issues of gender stratification within romantic texts if those issues are shaped and determined by the quantifying relations of capitalism? Does it not mean, too, that that silence precludes romanticism from presenting a utopian vision of women's freedom from the oppressive authority of patriarchy? Does it not, finally, render moot any feminist effort to discover and elaborate the possible contributions of romanticism to the oppression of women? Clearly, if Sayre and Lowy's account of romantic utopian thought is to be comprehensive and credible, it must recognize the absolute necessity of feminist intervention and revision.

But even if it acknowledges this necessity, there remains the question of how Carter's particular argument about capitalism and sexual violence may be integrated into a theory of romantic visionary idealism without denying the utopian core of Sayre and Lowy's argument. One answer, which may be embarrassingly simple, is that Sayre and Lowy are surely correct in recognizing the "positive aspects,"[31] or utopian dimension, of romanticism but entirely wrong in describing romantic utopian desire in unproblematic and essentialistic terms. As a fully realized historical materialist theory must acknowledge, the romantic rejection of capitalist values is not free of those values; it is, in fact, by virtue of its own historicity, at every turn mediated by the pressures and realities of industrial capitalism itself, especially by the commodifying and reifying tendencies within capitalism. Given this fact, to draw too absolutely the analytic distinction between romanticism and the bourgeois world order that romanticism would reject is to risk eliding the shaping and defining material conditions of romanticism itself.[32] While this explanation may at first appear to be intellectually too simple, it is, from a *historical* point of view, persuasive, for it insistently calls attention to the ineluctable social and historical mediations that both empower *and restrain* romantic visionary idealism in its effort to transform the world from a cold and alienating place into a more satisfying place of human pleasure and possibility.[33]

Once it is accepted that the quantifying processes of capital are always already present in the very interior of romantic desire, the controlling relations between gender and romantic utopian thought become subject to a more persuasive explanation: in British romanticism, at least, canonical romantic texts too often purchase their dream of a better world at the expense of women. Utopia, romanticism seems to say, is for men only, and the role of women—of Coleridge's "damsel with a dulcimer"; of Wordsworth's Dorothy; of Shelley's Emily, in *Epipsychidion;* of Byron's Astarte—is, at best, to inspire or to help locate the masculine vision of that utopia. In short, when Sayre and Lowy sort out too finely the romantic imagination from relations of capitalism (and gender) and identify that imagination as a guide to human betterment, they overlook a large and determining part of the material history of the late eighteenth and early nineteenth centuries that is not liberating.

To restate the problem somewhat differently, what Sayre and Lowy correctly recognize as fundamentally transformative and positive about romanticism are its insistence that, under the authority of industrial capitalism, the world is disturbingly inadequate and its many expressions of belief and hope that an alternative world can be constructed. But, as Carter's analysis persuasively shows, such recognition and desire can be formulated and played out only within the historical constraints of the world that have generated them: there is neither "an irreducible human universal" nor a "locationless area outside history" where the romantic utopia can be realized.[34] For this reason, the positive aspects of romanticism that Sayre and Lowy rightly admire can never be disentangled entirely from the historical conditions that determine them. Rather, they must be redefined and relocated within the horizon of history, which includes the fundamentally interrelated realities of capitalism and gender during the romantic period. Romantic visionary idealism must be examined within the context of the assumptions and values that undergird, energize, and delimit hope for human betterment, and those assumptions and values, in turn, must be investigated to determine how they are appropriated by, and inscribed within, romantic works of the imagination.

In other words, the precise intersections of history and utopia in the romantic imagination are necessary objects of inquiry in a historical materialist analysis of romanticism. And, as Carter's argument forces us to acknowledge, investigation of these intersections must at some point address not only the triumph of industrial capitalism but also the powerful importance of relations of gender—even in their ugliest manifestations—to the romantic imagination. More particularly, critical investigation must consider why romantic utopian thought, in rejecting the quantifying values of industrial capitalism, tends to be masculine in its formulation and fuels its hope for a better world with varying kinds of explicit and implicit injustice against women. While the romanticism that Sayre and Lowy admire may express real human need and desire for a different and better world, it cannot lead the way to that world until it has acquitted itself of the charges of sexual violence that Carter's analysis of sadism as cultural expression within the same historical moment obligates us to bring against it.[35]

Although the line of argument here would seem to be calculated to provide grounds for dismissing the argument of Sayre and Lowy—as well as the utopia for which romanticism longs—as just another masculine fantasy, this is not the case. Sayre and Lowy's argument is crucial to any effort to rethink romanticism from a historical perspective, and for several reasons. First, it elaborates, with great erudition and persuasiveness, the absolute importance of industrial capitalism in the rise of romanticism. Second, in defining romanticism as a response to industrial capitalism, the Sayre-Lowy argument provides a means of defining, defending, and advancing certain transformative energies within the romantic imagination. Finally, its emphasis on reification helps to elucidate the precise elements of a romantic desire for human expression in a world where an ever widening sphere of human experience is being reduced to commodities.

If the romantic dream of a better world cannot be accepted exactly on the terms set down by Sayre and Lowy but must be situated differently within the contexts of history, neither should it be dismissed too quickly; for it does begin, however slowly and problematically, to carve out a space within the powerful, reductive, and quantifying relations of industrial capitalism where the possibility of human control over human history can be imagined. The shock and cynicism of awakening in a world where even human flesh is a commodity to be exchanged on the open market can be transformed into righteous indignation only by an imagination strong enough to discover that other realities are possible.

For these reasons, Sayre and Lowy are right to insist upon the positive political importance of romanticism.

The historical materialist explanation of romanticism, therefore, cannot afford to abandon the very important work of Sayre and Lowy by claiming bluntly that it is insufficiently attuned to—and indeed blocks— the efforts of feminism. It must, rather, expand and develop the most fruitful lines of their argument, bringing into discussion what they have omitted: the necessary links, within the large and determining structures of capitalism, between the romantic utopian imagination and such matters as women's oppression, sexual violence, class struggle, and commodity exchange.[36] An effort in this direction can be energized by appropriating Carter's materialist analysis of sexual violence in a way that would expose the bourgeois masculinist logic informing the romantic imagination while at the same time enlisting that disclosure in the romantic cause against the bourgeois worldview—and against the economic realities behind that worldview.

7.

Interweaving the Sayre-Lowy and Carter analyses into a materialist feminist critique of romanticism entails several obvious but important preliminary steps. The effort must begin, as I have suggested, by denying outright the Sayre-Lowy assertion that romanticism is *essentially* antibourgeois as well as their assumption that the romantic utopian vision is unproblematic. In these regards, their argument is ahistorical, and plausible only when the category of gender goes unacknowledged. When a historically motivated gender analysis along the lines of that offered by Carter is appropriated by a historical consideration of romanticism, it becomes immediately clear that gender stratification is one of the hidden, and enabling, historical energies within the romantic imagination. Even as, at the level of surface structure, the romantic imagination would resist (as Sayre and Lowy claim) the quantifying pressures of industrial capitalism and the contradictions and oppression inherent in capitalism, at its deepest levels that imagination duplicates some of the quantifying procedures of capitalism by transforming women (who are poetically drawn in various descriptive and symbolic forms) into objects that, in turn, serve as the basis for utopian vision. The class struggle is thus played out homologically between an active masculine subject and a feminine (usually silent) object, and the product that emerges from this unequal relation is, ostensibly, a fully integrated masculine identity. If this claim bears any truth at all, then Sayre and

Lowy's insistence that "romanticism is in its essence anticapitalist"[37] must be discarded.

Refusing to distinguish absolutely between romanticism and capitalism and collapsing the definition of romanticism into the analytic frame of capitalism, however, do not require discarding all essences, or absolutes, in historical inquiry. At the center of the Sayre-Lowy argument is the correct recognition of the powerful, reductive, and socially pervasive powers of industrial capitalism, which made its successful final surge toward mastery of the Western world in the late eighteenth century. If Sayre and Lowy are correct in their claim about industrial capitalism (and I believe that they are), then capitalism must be seen as the *totality* within which romanticism emerges. Romanticism may resist capitalism; it may be "a deep-seated revolt against" the bourgeoisie;[38] but it is nevertheless always burdened by the demanding logic of capitalism and the bourgeois worldview that gives it cultural coherence.

In other words, to insist that romanticism be defined entirely within the context of capitalism does not necessarily mean that romanticism is reduced "to a bourgeois ideology"[39] or that it reflects, in a simple and direct way, only the values of the bourgeoisie. It may retain the politically important utopian energy that Sayre and Lowy claim for it, but that energy is nonetheless ideologically burdened with elements of the world it would transform or transcend—and the most readily apparent of those elements to materialist feminism, again, are gender stratification and the insistent reduction of the feminine to the status of object. To forget or deemphasize these absolute and quite real historical constraints on romanticism, even as a strong intellectual and political effort is made to preserve and advance romantic utopian thought, is to allow romanticism to hold in place certain contradictions that an antibourgeois definition of romanticism would reject. It is—stating the matter strongly—to risk transforming romanticism from a liberating political force into a conservative religious discourse whose primary function (or effect) is to elide and absorb the contradictions of the world as it is. For this reason, historical materialist criticism must insist upon exposing any retrograde bourgeois elements—such as gender stratification—embedded within romanticism and determine whether they are necessary or contingent and, if the former, what this might mean for romantic utopian expression.

What I am suggesting is that the Sayre-Lowy argument fails in two important ways, and precisely where Carter is strongest. First, although it advances a persuasive discussion of reification and of romanticism's response to reification, their argument does not consider the reifying processes operating within the romantic imagination itself, particularly in the area of gender relations. Second, and closely related, Sayre and Lowy do not offer an adequate theory of ideology, and thus their presentation of a romantic essence that is anticapitalist risks eliding constituent features of romanticism that are not anticapitalist and that, indeed, feed the energies of a developing bourgeois worldview. As I noted above, Carter's discussion of sadeian logic and violence as a transformation of feminine sexuality into a commodity, and as a cultural ethic that secures its authority (among other ways) by denying the historicity of commodities, provides a useful theoretical perspective for considering both of these matters. It thus can be used by materialist feminism to investigate the ideological blind spots of romantic desire (as well as the examples of explicit violence against women in romantic literature), to determine with greater precision the relations between romanticism and capitalism, and to explain the significance of those relations for relations of gender during the romantic period.

8.

I want now to consider the problem of romanticism and gender from a slightly different angle, one that perhaps relies more immediately on the critical contributions of poststructuralism than on the specific problematics of sadism. The aim here is not to shift the theoretical ground of discussion away from sexual violence and gender stratification onto textuality but rather to use the conceptual tools of poststructuralism to sharpen the focus on several issues central to the investigation of sexual violence in the romantic imagination and, further, to begin developing a suitable vocabulary for carrying out that investigation.

The materialist critique of gender in romantic literature can build upon the contributions of Carter by investigating romanticism's textual representation of the individual subject vis-à-vis its representation of women. Several simple questions suggest the importance of this issue. If the romantic imagination, even in its most revolutionary moments, reveals fundamental masculinist assumptions (as a quick glance at the work of Blake, Coleridge, Wordsworth, and Keats would suggest), and if its logic necessitates, or at least encourages, the appropriation and representation of a silent or dependent feminine other, then the question arises, as I suggested above, as to whether political feminism can or should retain any portion of the romantic project. Can the feminist deconstruction of the romantic masculine subject, in other words, clear a textual space for feminine identity within romanticism, or does romanticism constitute an authority that must be entirely jettisoned by an emancipatory feminist politics and criticism? If the answer to the first part of this question is yes, then what happens to romantic texts when the authority of the masculine romantic voice is displaced and a hitherto silent, or marginalized, feminine presence is accorded subject authority? In a feminist inscription of subjectivity, moreover, what happens to the sexual violence that a sadeian argument, such as the one offered above, may discover in the romantic portrayal of gender? Does it evaporate? Does it transfer to the feminized subject as one of its constituent features?

These questions can best be negotiated within the frame of the now common view that subject positions are both constitutive and constituted.[40] On this account, the imagining, masculine romantic subject must indeed be seen as an active agent in the construction of a feminine other and as therefore fully implicated in the oppression of and violence against the feminine other evident in many romantic texts. But the masculine subject is not a fully autonomous identity, driven only by its own inner logic; it is, rather, situated within a complex network of economic, political, and ideological (as well as textual and linguistic) constraints that both empower (and embolden) it and at the same time prevent it from reflecting fully upon itself. For this reason, its sincere expressions of ideal beauty, or of human possibility, can often be surrounded by images of violence (as in *Kubla Khan*) that bleed over onto the feminine vehicle of those expressions, locking the feminine within the contradictory and dangerous power of a highly developed masculinized world that is mistaken by the romantic imagination for utopia.

It is this inability of the masculine subject to reflect fully upon itself that enables a constructive feminist intervention into the bourgeois patriarchal features of romantic visionary idealism. That is, despite its *assumption* of autonomy, the masculine subject is in fact highly mediated, itself constructed within a social, historical, textual, and ideological frame beyond its full control. Thus it is often both right and wrong, free and unfree; its desire for unalienated existence, born as it is out of the confining and dehumanizing social conditions of industrial capitalism, is indeed admirable, though the shape of that desire can be sutured within historical expectations and realities that are hidden from view and that lead to the (at least partial) duplication of the very alienating and violent conditions that would be overcome. By situating itself politically and ideologically at this deeper level of conflict, which lies largely outside the reach of romantic intentionality, a materialist feminist critique can challenge and displace masculinist romantic logic while acknowledging the positive transformative values, desires, and hopes that appear at the level of expressive intention in romantic texts.

A materialist feminist critique of romanticism, on this account, would neither evacuate entirely the masculine subjectivity that constitutes a central part of the romantic imagination nor, more broadly, disregard romantic anticapitalism. Rather, it would decenter the masculine subject while at the same time engendering the feminine subject; and it would do so by broadening the historical grounds upon which the romantic imagination is formed, seeking to disclose and overcome the stratifications, injustices, and violence that too often energize that imagination, while preserving its most noble goal: a transformed society inhabited by freely creating, imagining individuals. The feminist deconstruction of the romantic subject, according to this program, would not follow poststructuralism into the textual fantasy world of free-floating and perpetually reconstituted subject positions within an ungrounded discursive chain but would rather imagine and seek to construct a world of free and autonomous subjects within the realm of historical necessity.

9.

The question of the subject and its importance to the feminist critique of romanticism perhaps becomes clearer when it is recast as a question about human agency.[41] While discussion of agency unavoidably repeats the logic of the discussion of subjectivity, it nonetheless is important because it helps to establish both the need for and possibility of feminist self-determination in the very masculine fields of romanticism and its critical reception.

It may be useful to begin by recalling that the romantic desire and nostalgia described by Sayre and Lowy are predicated upon the historical fact of fragmentation of community brought about by the rise of industrial capitalism and that the materialist feminist intervention into romanticism challenges the shape of that desire in the name of an emancipatory politics. This feminist intervention is complicated in part by the complex and ambiguous relations between the authoritative structures of romanticism and the strategies and motives of a critical response to it that seeks to determine its own fate. To put this difficulty in the form of a question: Can a feminist critical intervention be certain of its own identity and, more problematically, avoid duplicating the ideological structures of romanticism even as it claims that romanticism duplicates the ideological structures of the industrial capitalist world that it would reject? Or must it, on some deep level, inevitably remain defined by and contained within its object of inquiry?

The issue of agency can perhaps be best approached by acknowledging that the short (and perhaps unsatisfactory) answer to the above questions of whether feminist critique can avoid being absorbed into its object of inquiry is that it *must* avoid the pitfalls associated with romantic ideology; otherwise the feminist project collapses into yet another example of pluralism, becoming one view among many—with no special status—on a romanticism whose structures of authority are accorded the status of universals. The more properly intellectual answer echoes a point made above, namely that feminism can actively distinguish itself from romanticism, and can become politically liberating, through a dialectical and materialist form of critique that recognizes all human activity—even critical activity—as situated (textually, historically, ideologically), but always amid multiple and contradictory determinants that *produce* oppositional agents from the sheer weight and force of contradiction.[42] Such a dialectical critique can thus acknowledge the ontological status of romanticism while at the same time challenging romanticism's self-definition; it can, moreover, acknowledge the force of the humanist assumptions behind romanticism while reworking them both according to the historical situation of romanticism and of feminism; it can, in short, establish itself as an agent of interpretation and transformation *within* the historical reality of romanticism without being entirely subject to the authority of romantic ideology.

A general comment by Rita Felski on the dialectical relations between agency and structure helps to clarify the relations between romanticism and feminist critique that I am putting forward: "The relationship between structure and agency is dynamic, not static; human beings do not simply reproduce existing structures in the process of action and communication, but in turn modify those structures even as they are shaped by them. . . . Structural determinants both influence and are themselves influenced by social action and interaction."[43] As this comment suggests, the formative pressures of the world can never simply be denied, but they need not be seen as monolithic, either; they can and will be transformed even as they exert an undeniable shaping influence on human life. Similarly, the claim that romanticism makes on the feminist critique of it is real and undeniable, but it does not constitute a monolithic authority to be accepted or rejected wholesale. That claim, rather, is inherently contradictory, a fact that creates the possibility of a materialist feminist critique that is a transformative rather than purely destructive gesture, a critique that engages constructively with the object of inquiry even as that object limits and shapes critical activity.

While I am here stressing only the possibilities of feminist *critique,* the consideration of agency in fact must be broken analytically into two fields of investigation: the portrayal of things feminine within romantic texts and the feminist critical study of that portrayal. As I hope to show in subsequent chapters, the romantic feminine is often (though not always, as Byron's Gulnare and Shelley's Beatrice Cenci illustrate) more or less disempowered and locked into passivity by the authoritative structures of the masculine imagination—note, for example, Coleridge's portrayal of Christabel or of the damsel with a dulcimer, or Keats's portrayal of Madeline, or Wordsworth's portrayal of Dorothy in *Tintern Abbey*—while the imagining masculine ego appears as a universal expression of every dimension of human reality. But despite this seemingly fixed power relation, the romantic feminine constitutes a storehouse of historical knowledge, and hence possibility, that feminist critique can recover and use as a ground for advancing its own political and intellectual objectives, so that a powerless feminine on one level becomes the center of feminine empowerment on another as consciousness of gender stratification and oppression develops. As knowledge of relations of gender is recovered and assessed through historical investigation and critique, the passive romantic feminine becomes itself a voice against violence and oppression and thus a vital agent in the struggle for human liberation—both from romantic ideology and from the structures of authority (identified by Sayre and Lowy) that romanticism itself rejects. The problem of agency, then, is resolved as soon as critical investigation understands that the material conditions that determine the shape and limits of human activity also enable human activity. The violence of the romantic text contains within it the possibilities of its dialectical opposite—a world that is free of violence—and (as Carter argues with respect to sadism) produces the desire for that nonviolent world, as is seen not only in so many of the more noble romantic expressions of human integrity and hope for human freedom but also in the feminist disclosure of the partial, or reductive, character of the romantic imagination.

The line of argument that I am pursuing here maintains that representations of femininity in romantic texts (whether in descriptive or symbolic form) need not be viewed simply as a passive reflection of a transparent, static, and unitary masculine imagination. The feminine, rather, *necessarily* possesses subject possibility. Indeed, as I will argue particularly with respect to Wordsworth's *Tintern Abbey,* it is the subject capacity of the feminine other that makes it suitable as an object of desire and source of self-identity for the masculinist romantic imagination—but it is denied expression of that subjectivity by structures of authority that construct, secure, and extend bourgeois patriarchy. An important role of feminist critique is to map the ways in which those masculinist structures of authority operate within romantic texts and, in addition, to discover, in opposition to those structures, the grounds of feminine subjectivity and to construct the theory by which it can be advanced. Such a critical program assumes that, within the romantic text, the feminine subject is to some degree present though too often unseen and that the feminine voice speaks but is seldom heard; it assumes, in other words, that the feminine subjectivity present within romanticism can be liberated by, and in the form of, a feminist critique that challenges the oppressive, silencing, and often violent activities of romantic (masculinist) logic and imagination.[44]

The critical disclosure of feminine agency within romanticism constitutes a feminist appropriation and redefinition of romanticism. But, as I have shown, this disclosure does not—indeed cannot—reject entirely more traditional humanist explanations of romanticism. Rather it contends and demonstrates that those explanations, which in fact accurately describe romanticism's own understanding of itself, do not mean what they may appear to mean, that (as Byron said of Coleridge's metaphysics) the explanations themselves must be explained. Part of the explanation of romanticism and humanism, from a materialist feminist point of view, involves the insistence that methodological questions are also, on some level, substantive questions and, more specifically, that traditional humanist explanations and critical procedures have been one means of delimiting critical questions about romanticism and of controlling the kinds of intellectual issues suitable for investigation. Materialist feminism insists, in short, that humanism uses romanticism to political and ideological—as well as intellectual—effect. Materialist feminism also contests that use by showing that its own critical procedures and historical understanding have superior explanatory power and promise greater emancipatory possibilities than traditional humanist explanations of romanticism, which most often accept and seek to extend the romantic notion of a transhistorical redemptive power.

I want to stress that what I am describing—and advocating—here is not the sort of "Romantic feminism" that Rita Felski has rightly criticized. Romantic feminism, Felski says, assumes the existence of a subhistorical feminine sphere to which women can turn to discover self-identity and fullness of being. It "is the product of a psychological and aesthetic (rather than political) conception of liberation, less concerned with strategic means for ending the oppression of women than with expressing a paradisal longing for harmony fueled by a revulsion against the conditions of life under contemporary capitalism."[45] Such a view, in my estimation, would eventually duplicate the very violence that a materialist critique would overcome because, like both sadism and romanticism, it would look outside history for its meaning and thus leave uncontested, and untransformed, the contradictions and injustices of the world in which people actually live. What I am concerned with is not the elaboration of a romantic feminism but rather the materialist feminist critique of a fundamentally masculinist romanticism, a critique meant both to expose the gender stratification and violence that characterize many romantic texts and to elaborate the liberating possibilities for a political—and materialist—feminism as a result of that critique.

10.

This has been a rather long detour away from the specific issues of romanticism and sadism. But these arguments are important to the subject because they help to suggest the ways in which the sexual violence of the romantic text is caught in the larger problems of structure, society, and history. They also help to clarify my understanding of materialist feminism as a "goal directed" criticism—that is, as a criticism meant not simply to offer yet another interpretation of the romantic text but to elaborate a theory of literature and culture relevant to the cause of social transformation.[46] Deconstructing the masculine subject and engendering the feminine subject in the romantic text should not, of course, be mistaken for human liberation, but it may be seen as an effort in the direction of theorizing feminine subjectivity within a historical framework and of imagining how a world of free women and men might be achieved within that framework and what it might look like through the optic of a transformed romantic imagination.

The questions of agency, social structure, and subject construction, too, are important because they provide a useful vocabulary for discussing sadeian logic within romanticism without rejecting romanticism wholesale. Not only does this vocabulary deny outright the too simple and too frequent explanation that male aggression against women is "natural" or that romanticism *reduces* to masculinist logic; it provides a means of theorizing the cultural-historical grounds of the natural and thereby opens up the text to various interpretative possibilities. The romantic text can therefore be read against itself, dialectically rather than destructively, in a way that would expose its quiet or explicit violence while at the same time using the text as a historical record of unequal relations of gender and as a basis for building an alternative vision of human possibility.

As I hope I have made clear, the critical strategy that I am proposing, while indebted to certain movements within poststructuralism, seeks to carry out its constructive labors without reducing history and politics to their textual representation. As I have tried to present them, the issues of subject, structure, and agency are not textual matters alone; they are historical matters first that are appropriated and represented textually. The romantic portrayal of gender necessarily depends first not upon language but rather upon the decline of feudal, or aristocratic, patriarchy and the emergence of capitalist, or bourgeois, patriarchy, and it therefore is bound up with historical acts of violence and oppression. On this account, the sadeian underside of the romantic text is more than an element of the margins that can be used to deconstruct the expressed meaning of the text; it is a historical record of what was necessary in the development of a bourgeois patriarchal society—and necessary to the particular shape that the romantic utopian imagination took.

11.

Placed within the context of reification, ideology, class, and capitalist production—and within the poststructuralist context of subject, structure, and agency—Mario Praz's argument about the theme of the persecuted maiden in romantic literature, and about the particular significance of Sade to the development of that theme, becomes immensely complicated. For it now appears that the theme of the persecuted maiden, documented by Praz, involves much more than persecuted maidens alone and much more than the plot and theme of texts. It is a subject that extends beyond issues located purely at the surface structure of romantic texts to include issues that are entangled within a complex web of economic and cultural forces that Praz left entirely unexamined. The persecuted maiden, as the foregoing discussion suggests, is but a symptom, or a local textual moment—the moment that allows one to glimpse possible relations between romanticism and sadism—that can be *explained* only by reference to social relations and structures of authority that are as deep as history itself. The subject of the persecuted maiden cuts across modes of economic production into modes of patriarchal domination, forcing analysis of romanticism to shift its emphasis from literary history onto social history and to face directly the fact that the romantic utopian desire to overreach capitalism is never innocent, and that its guilt is too often gender-specific.

I want to stress finally that I do not wish to be understood as saying that romanticism is grounded *only* upon the subordination of women or upon various kinds of violence against women. As Sayre and Lowy, Jerome McGann, Marjorie Levinson, Marilyn Butler, and others have shown, romanticism emerges from multiple and highly complex determinants that cut across issues of class, psychology, economics, personality, and so on, as well as gender.[47] But gender is one crucial and determining component in the romantic situation, both in the world that produced romanticism and in the romantic expression of that world, and therefore, for political reasons, it must be tracked fully, both in an effort to locate and define its own constituent features and to explain its intersections with other social relations. This critical effort, moreover, must be carried out within the context of a larger historical materialist project—sketched earlier in this chapter—capable of situating and explaining both romantic portrayals of gender and the feminist critique of gender within romanticism. In other words, materialist feminism ought not to define itself as a special authority on interpretation of literary texts but should instead position itself as a point of leverage for social transformation. Only by finding its way both within and beyond the romantic text, I believe, can the primary objective of feminism—that is, human freedom—have any chance of succeeding.

In the following chapters, I want to examine selected poems by three canonical romantic writers—Wordsworth, Coleridge, and Keats—in the light of the theoretical speculations offered above. While other canonical writers of the period could have been selected for critical scrutiny, I choose these because they have been held in highest regard by traditional humanist criticism and thus are perhaps invested with a greater cultural significance than their counterparts. In addition, I make no effort to set these writers alongside female writers of the period, partly because Marlon Ross and Anne Mellor have provided excellent studies in this direction and partly because my aim is to make a theoretical and political point about the internal dynamics of canonical romanticism rather than to recover marginalized texts or to engage in a discussion about literary history.[48] Further, for the most part, I omit discussion of plot representations of the persecuted maiden because I want to concentrate on the historically specific *logic* of gender stratification that I have sketched above. While there are many scenes in romantic literature depicting sexual violence—in *Frankenstein, The Monk, The Cenci, The Brides' Tragedy*—that can be usefully compared to Sade's depictions of violence, these scenes do not constitute the core of my interest in romanticism and sadism. Rather than the undeniable fact of physical violence, I want to explore the common assumptions and logic shared by sadistic violence and romantic visionary idealism, in an effort to implicate romanticism fully in the historical conditions under which it was produced. Only by insisting that *all* of romanticism—from the texts portraying sexual violence to those articulating a strong and sincere desire for transcendence—shares the same historical ground as sadism will it be possible to explain (and appropriate for feminist purposes) romantic utopianism.

Chapter Two

Wordsworth

Recent critical investigations of gender relations in Wordsworth's poetry have spoken quite persuasively and emphatically about the powerful masculinist assumptions of Wordsworth's vision that refuse entirely to acknowledge—and, indeed, that overwhelm—feminine identity or autonomy. Two brief statements by Margaret Homans and Marlon Ross illustrate this point clearly. In writing about *Tintern Abbey*, Homans observes that Wordsworth "dominates the woman he addresses by his privileged discourse with nature, by the maturity of his imagination, and also by his masculinity."[1] Ross, writing about the same poem, observes that "Wordsworth in 'Tintern Abbey' exploits the feminine in order to forestall his confrontation with the ultimate rival, mortality."[2]

Although these comments are lifted from larger, complex arguments, they nevertheless indicate, among other things, the extent to which feminist criticism of canonical romantic texts feels compelled to abandon even the appearance of a neutral assessment of Wordsworth, adopting instead an aggressively interventionist stance. That stance insistently claims that the high moral aspirations of Wordsworth's great poem are constructed within a context of unequal relations of gender, which serve the interests of masculine identity while—and by—denying feminine identity and autonomy. Therefore, according to this position, whatever readers may wish to say about the *sincerity* of Wordsworth's vision or the *value* of the poem's depiction of moral possibility, his expressive *strategy* must be seen to rely upon ideas of domination and exploitation that raise serious questions about the place of women within the visionary scheme that Wordsworth describes.[3]

In what follows, I want to take the comments of Homans and Ross as a starting point for investigating relations of gender in *Tintern Abbey,* book 1 of the *Prelude,* and *Nutting.* As the comments by Homans and Ross suggest, feminist criticism has already taken a clear and strong stand on Wordsworth's poetry; nevertheless, I believe that it is possible—and necessary—to continue discussing, in a more detailed fashion than has yet been presented, the various dimensions and contexts of exploitation and domination that give the poetry its particular cultural importance. One aim of continuing the materialist feminist investigation of Wordsworth is to bring into critical view certain heretofore obscure or mystified currents of historical and social motion that both shape and energize his poetic vision, as well as the textual means by which those currents are gathered under the authority of the poet to be presented as universal truth. To proceed toward this critical goal is not to seek a kind of feminist conclusion about Wordsworth radically different from that drawn by Homans and Ross; it is rather to build upon previous feminist studies of the poet in an effort to elucidate the strategies, meanings, and social *logic* of exploitation and domination in his poetry. Extending and sharpening analysis in this manner gives additional historical weight and political force to the feminist critique not only of Wordsworth but also of romantic literature and culture.

1.

As Marjorie Levinson has shown in her brilliant historicist analysis of the poem, *Tintern Abbey* is an illuminating record of both the unstable social world of the early 1790s, when Wordsworth was a republican and, as Coleridge described him, at least a semiatheist, and the poet's desire to hide his personal involvement in the political events of that period. The poem registers a variety of complex social details and relations that inspired Wordsworth's youthful political hope, which quickly faded to severe despair, and articulates his effort to overcome despair by burying the past and constructing a vision of personal redemption grounded not in history but in nature and the imagination. According to Levinson, the poem is, in a very real sense, a deception in that it obscures the political and social issues from which it draws its greatest energy; but deception, as Levinson persuasively argues, can itself be used as an avenue into the social world of Wordsworth's imagination and thus should be seen as an important sign of the strategies deployed by the romantic ideology in dealing with that world.[4]

But the poem's social interest and historical energy ultimately reach beyond Wordsworth's personal life and the public events of the 1790s— that is, beyond the issues convincingly described in Levinson's argument. The poem's imaginative vision also embraces much larger, and slower, patterns of social motion. Although they cannot be reduced to, and are not even immediately recognizable in, the details of personal and public life, these patterns of social motion often shape those details in quite significant ways. The dimension of the poem's historical energy that I am describing can perhaps be best understood in terms of Fernand Braudel's argument that certain determining social currents abide at the "structural level" of history; that is, at an unseen and slowly changing but nevertheless decisive level of material reality, which undergirds the immediately recognizable and rapidly changing empirical details (such as those of Wordsworth's life or of the 1790s) situated at the "conjunctural level" of history.[5] While the energies, pressures, and forces operating at this deep structural level are not readily accessible to empirical analysis, they nevertheless possess powerful social and historical authority, the scope and nature of which are registered in cultural artifacts, among other places, dialectically enabling and often threatening to subvert expressions appearing on the textual surface of those artifacts. On this account, *Tintern Abbey* may be said to record not only the historical details discussed by Levinson but also a much larger historical and political unconscious, which governs an important level of poetic meaning, and, more generally, cultural expression itself.

One instance of the larger and slower pattern of social motion described by Braudel—and the one of greatest significance for the present discussion of *Tintern Abbey*—has to do with the transition, in Britain, from feudalism to capitalism.[6] As I argued in chapter 1, the emergence and triumph of industrial capitalism during the romantic period touched every corner of personal and public life and brought with it, among other things, a radical transformation of human consciousness itself, a transformation that reconstituted human identity in the extreme terms of subjectivity.[7] Placed within an interpretative framework that derives its explanatory power and takes its critical direction from the understanding of subjectivity in the romantic period as a historically determined phenomenon, *Tintern Abbey* yields socially significant meanings only remotely connected to Wordsworth's personal anxieties and hopes or to the specific political events of the 1790s. It becomes a poem, rather, in which meaning is no longer located at the biographical moment or at the level of authorial intention or even presence but on a ground constituted by the relations between specific

poetic details and certain powerful, if vague, deep-seated cultural assumptions and social currents—assumptions and currents marking the
sweeping transition from feudalism to capitalism.

From the perspective of the deep structure of social life, the political
inscriptions in *Tintern Abbey* take on an apparently contradictory
shape, quite different from that described in some recent historical
studies of the poem. For what on one level appear to be largely negative
and escapist patterns of desire—the calculated effort in the poem to put
the past under erasure; the effort to create a nonpolitical alternative to
the sordid social world that had lured Wordsworth into political activism—on another appear to be part of a *constructive* pattern of social
discovery, consistent with the steady successes and cultural demands of
industrial capitalism. While Wordsworth's repentance for his past sins
of political activism and his songful praise of a nature that might hold
the possibility of personal redemption may be informed by his backward look to a prepolitical world of unbounded human possibility that
has since been corrupted, at the same time they eagerly accept certain
fundamental portions of the new world order responsible for that
corruption—particularly those portions having to do with subjectivity,
individualism, and possessiveness. In short, in turning from politics to
nature, Wordsworth rejects the *public* commitments to social and political transformation while accepting and finding new life in the *ideological* components of that same transformation.[8]

As should be clear, I am not trying to situate *Tintern Abbey* amid
conflict (say) between aristocratic and bourgeois views on state government or even amid specific changes in the forces and relations of
production—though these are, of course, determining factors in the
transition from feudalism to capitalism. Rather, I am attempting to
describe the structural transformation—and the reduction—of human
consciousness under the increasingly authoritative quantifying pressures of large-scale political and economic change. While the transition
from feudalism to capitalism of course brought with it new and real
human freedoms (Wordsworth participated in and expressed his support of many of these freedoms), it also involved a remaking of people
from species beings into individual beings, the privatization of the
individual psyche, and the elevation of individual possessiveness;
Wordsworth did not escape the reality of this side of an emergent
bourgeois worldview. In a very real sense, Wordsworthian and romantic resistance to the newly triumphant political and economic authority
of industrial capitalism was made from *within* ideological frames of

reference that capitalism itself had created, so that romanticism's denial, for example, of capitalist political authority was fueled by a
commitment to and assumption of individual authority apart from
social life—by a commitment, that is, to structures of authority and
belief entirely consistent with the cultural demands and logic of capitalism.[9] Wordsworth's poetry generally, and *Tintern Abbey* particularly,
discloses this fact with remarkable force.[10]

The structuralist perspective I am advancing here, which focuses on
the construction of subjectivity within the emerging cultural authority
of capitalism, is important in a consideration of gender relations in
Tintern Abbey, for it enables one to understand that even while, at the
level of expressive intention, Wordsworth's imagination looks backward—or at least away from history—it in fact articulates a state-of-
the-art bourgeois ethic, one in which individual integrity appears to be
set forcefully against governmental and social corruption.[11] Further,
that integrity displays in strong form the masculine contours that are a
constituent part of bourgeois patriarchy; it is apparently an exception-
ally individualized, benevolent masculinity, which, in reality, achieves
its energy and definition from its highly socialized relation to a subordinated and silent feminine object. The poet's rush into nature's arms, in
this view, is not a simple escape from politics but rather an embrace of a
masculinist logic that is vigorously ideological and hence political; it is a
logic, moreover, that duplicates, at the level of ideology, the very ethic
of violence that the poet would escape by turning self-consciously away
from the world of public citizenship.

2.

The construction and operation of a subjective masculinist logic in
Tintern Abbey can be seen most clearly in the lines addressed directly to
Dorothy (111–59).[12] In these lines, Dorothy and nature are interfused,
as Wordsworth at once charges a feminized nature with human significance and naturalizes Dorothy to give her universal significance. While
this poetic maneuver, which interweaves the human with the pure truth
of nature, is an excellent example of romantic visionary idealism in its
most benevolent and hopeful formulation, at the same time it is charged
with the ideological energy of masculine desire shaped and directed
under the star of bourgeois patriarchy.[13]

The masculinist operations at the center of these lines are evident in
at least two ways. First, and most obviously, whatever these lines say
about the redemptive authority of nature, they establish the poet's

absolute mastery over the meanings and values associated with Dorothy. She is cast as the receiving object of his imaginative desire, and the various situations within which she is placed to demonstrate her receptivity signal the magnitude and ostensibly definitive authority of that desire. Dorothy is here a sign of the poet's former self; the human embodiment of nature's greatness; a dedicated soul whose attention and affection will always be dedicated to nature through the mediating presence of the poet himself: she is whatever the poet makes her, and she is worshipped for her permeability and responsiveness to the poet's imagination.

The poetic act of naturalizing Dorothy and feminizing nature, moreover, establishes an ideological space within which the poet's own masculine subjectivity can flourish. However idealistically they are portrayed, Dorothy and nature are always, ultimately, a frame within which the poet creates himself. His expressions of hope and moral integrity, and his conviction (described earlier in the poem) that he has found "Abundant recompence" (88) for all that has been lost through his past transgressions and through the ordinary processes of growing up, become possible within a psychological landscape colored by the energizing presence of Dorothy and nature, both of which inspire him (as the Dorothy passage shows) precisely to the extent that he exercises authority over them. Within the fresh and redemptive world that he imagines, they are the universal and human measures of his subjective identity and a validation of his authority insofar as their ideal qualities are assigned only by the poet himself. On this view, the poem's vision is inherently contradictory, as Dorothy and nature constitute a mastered space within which the poet sings himself into existence. To praise nature and Dorothy for their contribution to the poet's perception of his own stable identity, as the poem does, is not to transform them into a transhistorical redemptive presence, though the poet casts them as such, but rather to elide the ideological maneuver of their subordination and objectification.[14]

That the process of constructing a masculine subject position with power over a feminine idealized object is inherently an act of violence (or violation) is subtly disclosed in the poet's apparently friendly comment to Dorothy that

> . . . [I]n thy voice I catch
> The language of my former heart, and read
> My former pleasures in the shooting lights
> Of thy wild eyes. (116–19)

Beyond the obvious attitude of condescension here, in which Dorothy is cast as a virtual child standing before an adult authority, this passage hints at some of the darker energies governing the poet's relation both to Dorothy and to poetic composition. The word *catch* is particularly problematic in regard to those energies. At the literal level, of course, the poet probably uses the word to mean simply that he hears his own former language in Dorothy's voice. But the word suggests other meanings as well, which help to shape the particularly masculinist vision of the poem. For instance, in music a catch is a song. According to the *Oxford English Dictionary*, it is "a short composition for three or more voices, which sing the same melody, the second singer beginning the first line as the first goes on to the second line, and so with each successive singer; a ROUND. 'The catch was for each succeeding singer to take up or catch his part in time' (Grove)." In this case, the three singers would be Dorothy, the poet's former self, and the poet's mature self; and the mature poet catches "his part in time" from the voice of Dorothy, which had before taken up the voice of the poet's former self. On this view, *catch* calls attention to the form and process of songful, or poetic, expression in which the poet is engaged. In fact, in this definition, the word changes the interpretation of the passage entirely, making it appear not that the poet is simply hearing Dorothy's voice but rather that he is describing the poem itself: the poem is a song that uses the voice of Dorothy for the sake of idealizing and objectifying the poet's own former innocence ("my former heart"). According to this reading, Dorothy becomes a vehicle of expression for the poet's sense of his own coherent and cohesive identity over time.

The full significance of such a reading becomes clear in the light of yet another definition of *catch*: "to ensnare." This, in fact, is precisely what the poet's song does to Dorothy insofar as it enlists her voice in the poet's efforts to describe himself. Dorothy is caught in the poem and hence in the structures of ideas, values, and authority that are set down by the poet alone, with her presence and significance entirely dependent upon his authoritative song. Her voice is present, but only as a support for the poetic vision that has caught and transformed it.

Moreover, the poetic authority suggested by the catch that is a catch—the song that ensnares the voice of the individual being addressed—is enhanced by the poet's maneuvers to control interpretation. Dorothy is not only sung by the poet; she is "read" as well. The poet "read[s] / My former pleasures in the shooting lights / Of thy wild eyes." Following the contradictory poetic strategy that I have previously defined, the poet here casts Dorothy as both an inspiration for his singing and an object to be invested with meanings and values consistent with his self-identity. In other words, simply to be described as an ideal is insufficient; Dorothy must also be interpreted as such, for interpretation, the poem seems to suggest, draws energy from an object while at the same time seeking to point that energy in a quite specific, and ideologically interested, direction, that direction here being toward identity construction.

While textual interpretation, or reading, is a powerful form of control, it is also a more complex, and risky, task than singing, for it may call into play various, often contradictory, semiotic possibilities that would resist a reader's interpretative intentions. *Tintern Abbey* interestingly reveals the anxiety arising from such possibilities. In the very act of idealizing her and singing her virtues the poet betrays his anxiety (as John Barrell has argued) that Dorothy-as-text will somehow elude his masterful interpretative strategies and escape the role that he has designed for her.[15] That fear is hinted in the fact that, even as he sets her up to be read as a symbol of his early innocence, he articulates his anxious desire that she remain fixed as a stable representation of meanings that he has assigned to her:

> Oh! yet a little while
> May I behold in thee what I was once,
> My dear, dear Sister! and this prayer I make,
> Knowing that Nature never did betray
> The heart that loved her. (119–23)

Aware that Dorothy, rich in meaning for him, threatens to escape—after "a little while"—the interpretative controls placed on her, the poet attempts to lock her ever more securely into an immutable cultural and ideological landscape. He grafts her firmly onto nature in this passage—following a procedure that leaves the poet himself, yet again, at the center of all definitional authority ("what I was once")—in a maneuver that would make her a permanent, vital, and universal object capable of carrying the full range of meanings that his "reading" would assign to her.

The strategy of collapsing Dorothy and nature into one another as a way of situating them under a fixed poetic authority and investing them with meaning forms only one part of the poet's project of identity construction. This strategy is accompanied by a tribute to Dorothy that is at the same time a description of the power and authority of the poet himself. In the opening 111 lines of the poem, which describe the poet's

development toward "moral being," nature is assigned a virtually autonomous life, and the poet eagerly draws upon its energies for his own
moral and imaginative nourishment.[16] Once he achieves his goal of
expressing a moral vision (102–11) and begins to humanize and extend
that vision in the portrayal of Dorothy, the apparent autonomy assigned to nature is replaced by the autonomy, or centrality, of the poet
himself. Every detail from line 134 on describes the poet's sincere hope
that Dorothy will one day reap the rewards of life that he has previously
received; and yet these descriptions of hope do not allow Dorothy a
direct experience of nature at all comparable to the poet's own, described in earlier sections of the poem. Rather, the happiness that he
imagines for her comes through her relation to him:

> . . . [I]f solitude, or fear, or pain, or grief,
> Should be thy portion, with what healing thoughts
> Of tender joy wilt thou remember me,
> And these my exhortations! (143–46)

Or again:

> . . . Nor will thou then forget
> That after many wanderings, many years
> Of absence, these steep woods and lofty cliffs,
> And this green pastoral landscape, were to me
> More dear, both for themselves and for thy sake! (155–59)

One need not question the sincerity of the sentiments expressed here
to recognize that these descriptions refuse to Dorothy what the poet has
already claimed for himself and that, in fact, they constitute a *reduction*
of Dorothy to a complement of the poet's identification of himself as a
worshipper of nature. As the necessary medium through which Dorothy
must pass in finding the rewards that nature has to offer, the poet
becomes an exalted figure, while Dorothy's hopes and desires, which
are defined first by the poet and only secondarily by nature, become a
validation of that exalted status.

This poetic characterization of Dorothy entails a subtle reversal of
logic that obscures the ideological interests undergirding the expression
of hope and meaning in the poem, while at the same time—and thereby—
confirming the subject position of the poet. At the level of the poem's
surface structure, there appears to be a consistency of linear movement
wherein the poet, early on and through the auspices of nature, discovers
that he has access to the higher virtues and imaginative achievements of

life; once this discovery is made, he expresses his sincere hope that Dorothy will one day receive the same blessing that he has received. The poem moves outward from the individual to the world, with nature serving as guide and teacher. In fact, however, this linear development, as I have shown, is deceptive, because the poet's address to Dorothy in effect denies her the very subjective authority that had been a necessary component of his own hopes for redemption, converting her instead into nature, into the medium through which he had found his own redemption, so that his subjectivity is enhanced further even as hers is impeded. In the poem, she never enjoys the pleasure of self-discovery or of autonomous thought that the poet discovers in nature; she has only the pleasure of being attached to him.

The procedure that the poem follows here in its construction of masculinist identity also requires a kind of self-policing on the part of the feminine object. Even while one portion of masculinist subject construction entails what might be seen as violent manipulation—that is, the catching and reading of the feminine other—another portion requires feminine participation in the objectification of the feminine self; it requires, in other words, a willingness on the part of the feminine object to remain subordinate even in the absence of masculine authority. While Dorothy herself never explicitly displays that willingness, the poet interprets her as dependent upon him even in his absence when he says,

> . . . Nor, perchance—
> If I should be where I no more can hear
> Thy voice, nor catch from thy wild eyes these gleams
> Of past existence—wilt thou then forget
> That on the banks of this delightful stream
> We stood together. (146–51)

This passage extends and complicates an earlier passage in which the poet claims that, in years gone by, nature provided him with stable and nourishing guidance even at moments of hardship or loneliness:

> These beauteous forms,
> Through a long absence, have not been to me
> As is a landscape to a blind man's eye:
> But oft, in lonely rooms, and 'mid the din
> Of towns and cities, I have owed to them,
> In hours of weariness, sensations sweet. (22–27)

Even when nature was not immediately before him, he says, its redemptive energies guided and sustained him in much the way that the poet now hopes to sustain Dorothy even in his absence. On this logic, the poet's address to Dorothy secures for himself the authority that he had assigned before to nature; further, it claims for the poet a mobility that nature lacks; finally, the association of free movement and permanent authority, set against a naturalized and immobile Dorothy, intensifies her dependence upon him. This complicated rewriting of the earlier passage politicizes the poet's relation to Dorothy, for in this formulation she is made to look "naturally" to him for meaning, value, and hope, just as he had looked to nature before, thus proving that she is now and forever "catchable," in the various senses of that word.

To put this matter in slightly different terms, the distance between the poet's two references to catching-singing-ensnaring Dorothy might be used as a measure of his visionary authority over her. The first reference (116–19) is made in present tense—"thou art with me" (114)—suggesting an actual moment of physical attachment between Dorothy and the poet; the latter reference (148) imagines a future moment in which the absent poet retains and extends the authority established in the earlier passage. Dorothy, in the poet's imagination, becomes domesticated, accepting the idea that the poet is present to her even in his absence, and willing to find her role and value in her acceptance of that idea. The pattern of development here is similar to that presented in Keats's *Ode on a Grecian Urn*, in which the feminine is at once caught, belittled or sacrificed (in Tintern Abbey the belittlement is seen most readily in the poet's desire to "behold in thee what I was once" [120]), and then idealized in a process that effectively immobilizes the feminine, while the masculine subject is liberated for transcendental musings and physical mobility.[17] To the degree that nature (and, by extension, Dorothy) is the "anchor" of the poet's "purest thoughts" (109), then the poet himself is like a boat, free to move about in the comforting knowledge that his authority is permanent.

One additional relevant point about the last section of the poem involves the problem of the poet's relation to society and what that relation means in terms of his manipulation of gender. Here, as in earlier portions of the poem, society is portrayed in largely negative terms, as a corrupting influence from which the poet seeks to escape. Nature represents a place of retreat and an alternative to forms of social exchange:

> . . . for she [Nature] can so inform
> The mind that is within us, so impress
> With quietness and beauty, and so feed
> With lofty thoughts, that neither evil tongues,
> Rash judgments, nor the sneers of selfish men,
> Nor greetings where no kindness is, nor all
> The dreary intercourse of daily life,
> Shall e'er prevail against us, or disturb
> Our cheerful faith. (125–33)

The direction of this passage is toward an idea of presocial virtue and integrity, where the permanent structures of humanity rest protected and secure from the onslaughts of public life. But the passage does not advocate a denial of public exchange; it simply announces that in nature, and, again, by extension in Dorothy, can be found sources of strength that make public exchange bearable.

The gender dimension of the poet's attitude here is significant because it locks Dorothy into nature and away from the world that the poet himself takes for granted as being available to him, even if it is sordid, selfish, and unkind. The privatization of the feminine, in fact, is a necessary component of the poet's own mobility and optimism in a degraded world, and for this reason it is celebrated and idealized by the self-constructing masculine poetic voice. Dorothy is represented as pure, virtuous, and noble, because she is a human source within which the poet finds these characteristics that he himself would possess. The greater her possibility as an ideal, the greater the authority of his identity, because, as the poem states explicitly, all of her accomplishments are mediated by his strong presence.

3.

I want now to push this argument even further away from conventional understanding of the poem's expressed meanings to suggest that the logic I am describing here is historically connected—and remarkably similar—to the logic of pornography that traces back at least to Sade, whose major work appeared in the same decade as *Tintern Abbey*. To argue along these lines, of course, is not to suggest that Wordsworth the poet is engaged in malicious deceit or sadistic pleasure and that he in fact personally detests Dorothy even as he pretends to admire her. Rather, it is to say that the poem's vision of gender, like Sade's vision of human nature and human sexuality, participates in the cultural and social realities of its day—particularly in the assumption of the autonomy and authority of the masculine subject and the absolutely dependent status of femininity. It is also to insist that no vision, of either gender, self, or society, entirely escapes the social and historical conditions under which it is produced. In the late eighteenth and early nineteenth centuries, those conditions produced a cultural logic that is expressed sometimes as transcendental desire and at other times as a desire to exercise uncontrolled sexual violence; but the logic itself is similar insofar as it presumes in both extremes that absolute hierarchies of meaning are constitutive of human reality.

While virtually all of Sade's philosophy is cast in a vocabulary of lust and sexual violence, the logic behind that vocabulary, as I tried to show chapter 1, nevertheless extends to the full range of gender relations in bourgeois society, including those relations articulated by visionary romanticism. At the center of his philosophy is the viciously individualist assumption that "egoism is Nature's fundamental commandment" (604): "the philosopher . . . is alone in the universe, he judges everything subjectively, he only is of importance" (608). Sade's subjective philosopher, moreover, like the romantic visionary poet, is *always* masculine, and the free exercise of his intellect, imagination, and authority usually results in the diminution of the feminine object, a point that is viciously emphasized over and over in his many depictions of acts of sexual violence against women. In a particularly brutal description of the relations between husband and wife, for instance, he remarks: "The relationships of a wife to her husband and that of the chicken to myself are of identical consequence, the one and the other are household chattels which one must use, which one must employ for the purpose indicated by Nature, without any differentiation whatsoever" (646).[18] Such a perspective actively denies the human status of women and reduces them to objects whose value resides entirely in the ease or pleasure with which they may be manipulated and consumed by men.

Recent radical feminist investigations and theories of pornography recognize the social and structural significance of this sort of pornographic logic. What makes pornography, and particularly sadistic pornography, so abhorrent to these writers is not so much the sexually explicit nature of pornographic material; it is rather the violent hierarchy of gender relations portrayed in that material—that is, the structure of assumptions that charge sexual acts of violence with meaning. Donald Alexander Downs's summary of the radical feminist view of pornography is helpful in clarifying this structural issue: "Pornography socially constructs women's subjectivity in a manner which makes them objects of male pleasure and power and strips them of their own autonomy. Thus, pornography is an ingredient in the pervasive patriarchal silencing of women's voices and beings."[19] Pornography both constructs and registers the oppression of women, and its evil lies in this fact rather than in its explicit portrayal of sexual acts or in the moral issue of obscenity.

The importance of this view is, in part, its insistence that sadism and pornography are not cultural aberrations but rather explicit representations of certain deep-seated structures and relations of authority governing all questions of gender in modern society. That is, sadism and pornography embody and reflect relations that are systemic in the culture rather than individual, and, in their explicit commentaries, they reinforce those relations; they are both a sign of masculine authority and a process by which that authority is validated and extended. Therefore they can and should be set alongside more conventional or reasonable or palatable portrayals of gender as a way of determining and illuminating the underlying assumptions and structures of authority governing those portrayals.

Sade's views, along with the radical feminist critique of sadism and pornography, go a long way toward providing a vocabulary for discussing bourgeois relations of gender as they are portrayed in such works as *Tintern Abbey,* for, as extreme expressions of a pervasive cultural reality, they encourage critical consideration of the logic of gender apart from notions of authorial intention or cultural self-definition. They encourage individuals, that is, to think in terms that derive from notions of the structural determinations of individual life. And while sadeian and (in my view) some radical feminist theory are ultimately limited by their shared assumption that the pornographic, violent, and sexual subordination of women results from tendencies within the essential nature of the male (Sade defends that alleged nature, while radical feminism condemns it),[20] both positions offer highly persuasive *descriptions* of the logic governing what I consider to be historically and culturally specific relations of gender, relations that, as I have tried to show, arise with masculine subjectivity under the pressure of industrial capitalism.

The usefulness of Sade in a materialist feminist investigation of such mainstream canonical works as *Tintern Abbey* is perhaps most readily apparent in the similarities between Wordsworth's vocabulary of nature and Sade's. Both writers rely upon a single concept of nature to authorize and explain their very different visions: for Sade nature is both human nature and objective, or physical, nature, and both are identified most fundamentally in terms of masculine authority and feminine subordination; for Wordsworth, nature is also both human nature and objective nature, though both are characterized by claims of benevolence and moral integrity lacking in Sade. Moreover, these uses of nature are equally masculinist, though Sade's masculinity is violent while Wordsworth's is apparently nonviolent. Both portrayals place a masculine subject at the center of nature and as the embodiment of, and spokesperson for, nature's meaning, even as nature is feminized (in the passage quoted above, for instance, Sade equates woman with a chicken, while in the final fifty lines of *Tintern Abbey* Wordsworth feminizes nature). In short, whether nature is cast in benevolent or violent terms, it is made to represent an absolute and socially unmediated justification for the masculine subject's identification of himself in opposition to an objective, and mastered, world.[21]

A final issue regarding *Tintern Abbey* may be raised but not satisfactorily resolved at this juncture. If the poem's logic is sadeian in nature, then on what positive grounds may the poem be read, studied, and admired, especially by feminists? A satisfactory answer to this question would entail several considerations. First, at the level of critical strategy, the poem is important to a historical materialist feminism because it reveals in interesting ways the dialectical center of hierarchical relations of gender. Even as the poem presents a powerful masculine identity, it shows the extent to which that identity depends upon a particular relation to femininity. That necessary relation suggests that masculine identity is not entirely autonomous insofar as it must be validated by a silent other, and thus that femininity possesses the hope, or possibility, of its own identity. Dorothy may be silenced in the poem, but she does possess a voice, and that voice, in its very silence, speaks against the purely masculinist claims made by the poet and on behalf of another possible vision. In other words, Dorothy's presence in the poem is not only a sign of masculine authority but also a sign of its potential disruption.[22]

Further, the poem does not *reduce* to sadeian logic (at least as sadism is generally and most simplistically understood) even if its vision of gender reflects that logic. Beyond all logic, the poem expresses real human hope and desire, which possess at least some portion of the integrity claimed for them by its poetic voice and by traditional criticism alike. Moreover, despite the poem's masculinist assumptions, its expres-

sions of hope and desire are not entirely selfishly masculine insofar as
they imagine a better life for Dorothy as well as the poet. To reject the
vision of the poem entirely, therefore, would not only be to reject its
violent logic; it would be tantamount to rejecting as well its vision of
human betterment for men *and* women—that is, to reject the poem
entirely is to reject as well the goal toward which feminism strives.

But, as the foregoing analysis demonstrates, the poem's integrity and
vision of hope are not innocent, and this is the second point that must
be understood in trying to find a feminist means of recuperating it.
While the sadeian logic manifested in *Tintern Abbey* does not entirely
destroy the poetic vision of human betterment, it does force the poem
and its interpretation away from all purely spiritual or transcendental
explanations of that vision and into the hard confines of history, culture, and society. It is in the rich and complex picture of these historical
constraints that the poem's positive importance for feminism resides. By
looking beyond the poem's ideological commitment to a transcendental
redemptive authority to the material contexts within which human
desire for moral integrity is expressed, feminist deconstruction transforms *Tintern Abbey* from a mystifying statement about spiritual redemption into a poetic historical record of the complexity, contradictions, and possibilities of human life itself. In this view, exposing the
poem's sadeian logic, upon which bourgeois gender relations are constructed, is a necessary step toward recuperation, one that does not
destroy hope or desire but rather begins the constructive process of
identifying a feminine reality within the romantic imagination. Though
it may be oppressed and exploited, that reality enriches the poem by
particularizing its complicated human dimension and elucidating its
importance as a register of historical knowledge. In short, investigation
of the poem's masculinist character enables a feminist project to work
beyond mystifying (though sincere) expressions about human life and
begin, however tentatively, to understand hope in terms less burdened
by unequal relations of power.

It may be appropriate, before proceeding, to state that in subsequent
chapters I attempt to elaborate this view by investigating from a slightly
different angle the internal dynamics of poems to show how sadeian
logic is challenged even as it is articulated. While my primary concern is
to elucidate the violent procedures whereby a masculine poetic identity
is constructed, I also want to consider, particularly with respect to
Coleridge's poems, the anxiety and uncertainty surrounding the sadeian
logic upon which romantic expression seems to rely. In that anxiety and

uncertainty—for example, in a poem like *Christabel* or even *Eolian Harp*—can be found an inchoate feminine identity, which may be disruptive or even ostensibly demonic but which nevertheless repeatedly forces into view the problematic status of romantic visionary idealism and thereby forces romanticism to contend with, and occasionally even to seek accommodation with, women and history. While Wordsworth's poetry seems to be less vulnerable than Coleridge's to an intrusive feminine identity, it nevertheless reveals a similar dynamic insofar as it relies upon a particular portrayal of femininity in its portrayal of masculine vision, and (as I have suggested) in so doing, it creates the possibility of feminizing hope in the romantic imagination.

Some of the issues being traced here involving the construction and expression of bourgeois patriarchy can be elaborated by reference to book 1 of the *Prelude*. I do not wish here to offer a detailed analysis of the *Prelude* but rather to comment briefly on several matters having to do with gender relations that extend, and that I hope will clarify, the way capitalist cultural authority, sadeian logic, and romantic visionary idealism intersect in and enliven Wordsworth's poetic vision.

Perhaps the most significant scene in book 1 for the purpose of understanding its specific assumptions about gender is the boat-stealing episode (1.357–400).[23] In some respects, this scene describes in more urgent terms than *Tintern Abbey* had done the social and psychological turbulence marking the reconstruction of patriarchy under the competing pressures of aristocratic and bourgeois worldviews, for the weight of its statement falls upon the poet's confrontation with nature rather than upon the transparent structures of nourishment and support in nature, which had occupied him in the earlier poem. In the boat-stealing episode, the poet portrays his youthful experience on a landscape of social and psychological activity that threatens him and then challenges him to convert that threat into a triumphant moment of self-identification; the self-identification that the poet attempts to bring to life, in turn, may be specified as uniquely bourgeois.

It is commonly recognized that the boat-stealing episode contains within it a symbolic description of masturbation, or at least that its psychology may be read as analogous to the psychology of masturbation, and it is at this level that the problem of gender may be proposed first. To understand what sort of gender issues are at stake in reading the scene in the context of a psychology of masturbation, we must recall certain images from other scenes. In a passage immediately preceding the boat-stealing episode, the poet, after lamenting his inability to discover a suitable subject for a long poem, looks for and finds comfort from his distress in the soothing "voice" (1.273) of the Derwent river. This river, he goes on to say, receives "On his [the Derwent's] smooth breast the shadow of those towers / That yet survive, a shattered monument / Of feudal sway" (1.283–85). This historical allusion appears again in the boat-stealing episode, where the image of the tower is repeated, only this time in a sexually suggestive way, so that the troubled energies of history, nature, and sexuality are associated. Describing his rowing activity in the boat and the responsiveness of the natural landscape (in the form of the mountain) to that activity, the poet states:

> . . . I struck and struck again,
> And growing still in stature the grim shape [of the mountain]
> Towered up between me and the stars, and still,
> For so it seemed, with purpose of its own
> And measured motion like a living thing,
> Strode after me. (1.380–85)

When set against one another, these two images of the tower—one historical (feudal-aristocratic), the other natural (sexual-phallic)—mark the boundaries of the social and psychological motion registered in the poet's vision of his own powers in relation to nature. Specifically, the images suggest a historical tension and transformation that carry within them a sexual and ideological transformation. The demise of the feudal towers that the poet's beloved Derwent shadows forth is accompanied by the emergence of the poet's own phallic tower—similarly emblematized in nature, in the form of a mountain—which is generated by his own private, transgressive, and productive activity (rowing). And just as the "shattered monument" of one tower is nostalgically recalled, the rising authority of the other is feared even as it is admired, powerfully suggesting not only sexual anxiety but also (in the context of the poem as an autobiography of the poet's mind) the problematic status of an intensely personalized poetic imagination that is situated between declining and emergent historical and psychological energies.

As this formulation suggests, even in its anxiety-ridden condition, the poetic vision that Wordsworth struggles anxiously to describe is both pleasure-driven and emphatically masculine. The emergent phallic energy (evident in the imagery of the scene) that I am describing here as both frightening and at the same time exciting, enabling, and psychologically crucial is a sure sign that the poem's questions about gender are questions mainly about masculine identity. And in this respect, the *Prelude* follows directly the path of *Tintern Abbey* in putting forward an entirely masculinized understanding of identity.

But, as *Tintern Abbey* also amply demonstrates, even the narrowest questions about masculine identity must ultimately confront as well questions about the nature and situation of femininity, and it is precisely here—at the question of the feminine—that the boat-stealing episode becomes most compelling. For even as the imagery expresses a commitment to and desire for the power located in a newly discovered masculinity—

> . . . lustily
> I dipped my oars into the silent lake,
> And, as I rose upon the stroke, my boat
> Went heaving through the water like a swan (1.373–76)

—at the same time the episode reveals an interesting confusion about gender. Specifically, the masculine and feminine references cannot be entirely disentangled in such a way as to assure the pure masculinity of masculine sexuality and gender. For instance, one way that the episode is sexualized is through the reference to the boat as a *pinnace*, which may be a play on the word *penis;* and yet the pinnace is clearly feminized in Wordsworth's description—"She was an elfin pinnace" (1.373)—while oars are associated with the real sexual function of the penis ("lustily / I dipped my oars"). When one considers that the speaker is throughout cast in masculine terms (even while occasionally his mind is feminized), it becomes clear that what in fact is happening within the vocabulary of masturbation is that an overarching masculinity is being set in place *above* particular masculine and feminine characteristics that would be controlled.[24] Even so, as the guilt associated with stealing the boat suggests, the very necessity of a feminine principle within masculine identity becomes problematic, disturbing, and threatening.

To cast this matter in slightly different terms, part of the difficulty of understanding the boat-stealing episode resides in the fact that the act of masturbation suggested in the language of the scene is not only an act of masculine control and self-construction; it is also an act that demonstrates masculine dependence upon femininity as a source of sexual pleasure, and that dependence reveals debilitating psychological anxiety and fear. That is, the act of masturbation described in the scene is presented in terms of an autonomous masculine identity, but it is grounded, psychologically at least, in a notion of heterosexual pleasure as an appropriation and subjugation of femininity. (Not to ground masculine identity in this way, of course, potentially would entrap poetic expression in the psychological web of homosexual desire.) The strategies of masculinity and pleasure are seen, for example, in the fact that the poet divides his youthful psyche into masculine and feminine components, with the penis being feminized even as its masculine authority is retained in the image of the oars. While this maneuver ostensibly secures the condition and definition of masculine identity, in fact it marks the limit of that identity because the masculine sexual pleasure described in the scene requires a feminized other, which is acknowledged even as it is made to appear absent. In real terms masculine identity is dependent, and its apparent autonomy is in fact isolation. The male psyche, in this scene at least, reveals its own dubious status and consequent sense of dread. The realization of the limits of masculine identity, imagination, and authority, in fact, produces a psychological state so disturbing that the poet has his youthful former self entirely give over the secret pleasure path he has been following and return the boat to its proper "mooring-place" (1.388), in effect abandoning his exploration of male-centered sexuality. The complex and contradictory conditions of masculine identity are glimpsed and even approached, and yet they are never mastered, leaving masculinity in an awkward state of mystery and fear as well as confused desire.

Another feature of the episode that helps to clarify the historically specific significance of gender relations involves the plot-level act of theft. One central question about the historical emergence of masculinist logic and bourgeois patriarchy involves their relation to the bourgeois vision of private property. In the boat-stealing episode, this question is posed in the intricate relations of the plot-level description of theft, the symbolic representation of the theft as an act of masturbation, and the turbulence of gender within that act of masturbation. The relations between these levels of the text can be at least partly understood in terms of the poet's ultimate acceptance of the right to private property, which is demonstrated plainly when he returns the stolen boat to the spot from which it was taken and feels duly chastened for having taken it at all. At the same time, the boat itself is feminized, which is to say that the feminine other in the episode is synonymous with private property. Just as from a sexual-psychological perspective a feminine other is called into play to enable masculine sexuality and identity, so the feminization of private property demarcates the bounds of masculine identity. The boat is not returned out of any acknowledgment of or respect for the feminine but rather as acknowledgment of a line of difference between the masculine subject as agent and the feminine object as a property upon which that agency is carried out. Called into play only to be returned to "her mooring-place," the boat, then, signifies a paradox: it suggests both the respected and necessary presence of private property within the sphere of bourgeois reality as well as the necessary and subordinate position of femininity, *as property,* within the sphere of bourgeois masculinist logic. *As property,* the feminine can be appropriated and put in the service of masculine identity, but property itself remains a sacred cornerstone of bourgeois reality. In focusing the social logic of private property in this manner, the poem draws a clear line between "those towers / That yet survive, a shattered monument / Of feudal sway" (1.283–85) and the bourgeois social and psychological terrain that the poet's youthful self attempts to learn.

One way book 1 of the *Prelude* accommodates and validates its own masculinity is through homosocial expression that finds authority in a larger masculine presence, which helps to locate and pin down certain feminine energies and principles that are both necessary and (as the boat-stealing episode shows) threatening to masculine identity. A homosocial expressive strategy is necessary because, even as the poet in book 1 of the *Prelude* consistently presents his voice as masculine, he is compelled by the logic of bourgeois masculinity to present his own mind in feminine terms; and he tends to feminize nature as well, presenting it as a feminine teacher that in turn is nurtured and mastered by the masculine voice and presence of the poet. Such descriptive strategies, as I have shown in my discussion of the boat-stealing episode, create gender confusion because masculine identity can never entirely establish its autonomy vis-à-vis a perfectly defined feminine other, even though it takes autonomy as the essential ingredient of masculinity.

The homosocial expression that seems calculated to resolve the sort of confusion and anxiety seen in the boat-stealing episode is evident at the highest level of the text, which is consistently presented as an address to Coleridge. Standing outside and above all particular narrative episodes, the figure of Coleridge represents a fixed masculine presence, which validates the poet's quest for his own (masculine) poetic identity. That quest takes him through a landscape of aristocratic and bourgeois tensions, which, in their turn, press down hard on psychological and political matters having to do with the emergence of subjectivity and its problematic gender dimensions. By using the figure of Coleridge as a constant reference point (see, for instance, 1.46, 134, 618), the poet assures that, however confused his poetic representations may be with respect to gender—note, for instance, his feminized mind or his feminized penis—his own identity, finally, is unequivocally masculine, tied ineluctably to the perdurable character of the absent yet ever present Coleridge. By constructing Coleridge as his primary audience, Wordsworth effectively masters problematic issues having to do with the real relations between masculinity and femininity by making the poem first and last the story of one man speaking to another.

According to this perspective, one underlying assumption of the narrative being presented is that, while things feminine may be desirable and even necessary, they must ultimately be controlled and situated by masculine agency. The boat as female principle may provide a momentary secret pleasure, but it must finally be returned to its proper place in hiding, and its full significance pondered carefully; feminized nature may indeed be a teacher, but it must finally be subject to the poet's shaping voice; and the poet's own feminized mind may have energies of its own, but they must finally be brought under the control of masculine identity and poetry. As the poet remarks at one point about his mind:

> . . . [H]is [the poet's] mind, best pleased
> While she as duteous as the mother dove
> Sits brooding, lives not always to that end,
> But like the innocent bird, hath goadings on
> That drive her as in trouble through the groves. (1.139–43)

Such tensions and pressures persist through the book in a way that can never be satisfactorily resolved at the level of philosophy, in which Wordsworth seems to be primarily interested; but they are always resolved at the level of ideology insofar as the poet finds his durable reference point in a masculine identity that he projects above all narrative particulars, and that absorbs the apparent contradictions in those particulars in a way that transforms them into small difficulties to be sorted through by a coherent masculine subject.

The structural dimensions of bourgeois masculine identity that are delineated and constructed in book 1 may be elucidated by reference to Jean-Joseph Goux's discussion of feudal-aristocratic and capitalist-bourgeois libido. In specifying the historical parameters of libido, Goux situates feudal-aristocratic libidinal energy within the frame of a "consumption economy" and bourgeois libidinal energy within the frame of a "revenue economy," arguing that, within each, it is *wealth* that assigns qualitative value to sexuality. This means, among other things, that feudal-aristocratic sexuality is necessarily aligned with use value, while bourgeois sexuality is identified with exchange value. Goux explains his position in this way: "The feudal subject of *jouissance* is the subject of dissipated wealth, of impetuous and unproductive consumption. He realizes himself . . . only in monstrosity, in caprice, in arbitrary and bizarre whims. In his arrogance and scorn, in the very act of considering the labor of other men, the blood that is sweat by slaves or serfs, as the prey of his desire, he knows the men themselves as sacrificed, nullified beings and thus knows himself as one." Bourgeois libido, on the other hand, is "sober, thrifty, prosaic, subordinating jouissance to production and finding it only through calculation in the economy of savings and earnings, of credit and debit, accompanied by an exact accountability of goods and rational use of time." In other words, feudal libido consumes "more than it possesses," while bourgeois libido postpones consumption, finding pleasure instead in the *calculation* of pleasure that is imagined to be possible with the accumulation of wealth.[25]

Moreover, according to Goux, the bourgeois postponement of jouissance—the pleasure that arises from the contemplation of pleasure—finds its purest sexual expression in masturbation, as this sexual act alone would seem capable of appropriating, while at the same time rising above, the pressures and contradictions that characterize the world of exchange value. Sexual self-absorption, that is, becomes both a sign of individual authority and identity—a sign of the private pleasure in the calculation of private wealth—as well as an anxious (symbolic) register of the alienating and even frightening social processes of accumulation. The postponement of jouissance, therefore, while marking the authority of the individual subject over the process of accumulation and conditioning the particular form of pleasure that derives from that authority, at the same time is a mark of social and psychological isolation and fear.

Such a perspective on the historical determinants of sexual energy helps to elucidate the boat-stealing episode by focusing both the poet's relation to nature and his imaginative appropriation and definition of private property. One clear aim of the poet, for instance, is to accumulate a store of images and lessons from nature that can provide a solid ground for poetic identity. The accumulation of nature's wealth, moreover, includes the poet's developing sense of nature's property dimensions. When the poet steals the eggs from the nest of a mother bird in the scene immediately preceding the boat-stealing episode (1.326–39), he remarks upon his awareness that a transgressive act has been committed, though he does not explore and articulate its significance to his personal identity. When he steals the boat, however, the transgressive act presses him to a heightened awareness of his own character vis-à-vis that of nature. One important difference between the two thefts is the difference between a socially undemarcated natural wealth (the eggs) and a socially specific form of private property (the boat).

While the poet's different responses to these thefts might suggest that he is placing social wealth above natural wealth, what is more likely is that he is marking out the boundaries of personal accumulation by using the natural and the social as a binary opposition that is necessary to personal identity. That is, at least two social-psychological matters are in operation here: the poet articulates his right, or freedom, to take as he pleases from nature and understands his activity as a necessary part of his self-construction; at the same time, he must not take everything into himself—he must not immerse himself entirely in the grand wealth of nature—for to do so would destroy the distinctiveness and separateness that are essential to his *human* identity. Private property, in the form of the boat, therefore becomes important ideologically because it marks the human, or social, dimension of his own character: he must return the boat to its proper place out of respect for the distinction that makes his identity possible.

The calculation of the pleasures of wealth is grounded in deferral of the pleasures of wealth. The poet takes his measure of the boat and of nature, and in taking that measure he finds himself. The act of finding himself displays a spare economy wherein he knows the boundaries of accumulation—the contours and parameters of wealth—and discovers pleasure in that knowledge, while the wealth itself is always returned to its respected place to be contemplated by the calculating, pleasure-seeking individual identity. The lesson of the boat-stealing episode, in short, teaches the relations of natural wealth, private property, individual identity, and sexual pleasure. And all of these relations, as I have argued, are not simply bourgeois but patriarchal as well insofar as every experience is measured in terms of a specifically masculinist logic.

I want to mention, finally, the issue of guilt in the boat-stealing episode, for this issue provides an important ideological component in the construction of coherent identity that the poem carries out. Whether the passage is viewed as an allegory of masturbation, as a commentary on bourgeois private property, as an example of natural pedagogy, or as a combination of all of these, guilt figures prominently in the poet's presentation of his activity:

> With trembling oars I turned,
> And through the silent water stole my way
> Back to the covert of the willow tree;
> There in her mooring-place I left my bark.
> . . . .
> . . . [F]or many days, my brain
> Worked with a dim and undetermined sense
> Of unknown modes of being; o'er my thoughts
> There hung a darkness. (1.385–88, 91–94)

This description of the poet's guilt points directly to his own sense of the social dimension of his actions and suggests at least one of the ways by which social life is ideologically specified. For guilt both acknowledges the distinctions and boundaries that are necessary to bourgeois society and subjectivity and at the same time helps to resolve those distinctions and incorporate boundaries into a coherent, unified, individual subject: guilt is one means by which the poet knows himself in relation to the objective realities of private property, sexual desire, and gender; guilt supports individual (masculine) identity by forcing awareness of the private self within a larger frame of these realities, which are marked by distinction, division, and contradiction. The cultural function of guilt, in this view, is constructive, reinforcing the stable center of individual identity.

The boat-stealing episode helps to focus certain larger issues of book 1 of the *Prelude,* particularly those having to do with the production of poetry in an age of uncertain poetic identity; the relation between older poetic forms and standards and particular (bourgeois) assumptions and expectations pressuring poetic activity in Wordsworth's own day; the problematic nature of gender at a moment of social and historical upheaval; and the important, but also problematic, role of sexual desire in the poetic effort to negotiate these and other matters. If the episode can be reduced to coherent explanation, that explanation, I believe, must include commentary on the necessary relations between masculinity, sexual desire, declining feudal definitions of self, and the emergent and authoritative presence of private property; and it must bring these matters to bear on the production of poetry—and the construction of poetic identity—in an age of declining aristocratic sensibilities and emerging bourgeois energies. While the above analysis does not fully elaborate all of these issues, it does begin to sketch a conceptual and methodological framework within which the historical explanation of the *Prelude* can be carried out.

I want now to touch glancingly upon Wordsworth's *Nutting* in an effort to draw together some of the historically charged and gender-specific issues that I have been tracking above. It is appropriate to conclude a discussion of Wordsworth and gender with reference to this poem because it describes quite explicitly some of the sexual, social, and cultural energies that lie deep beneath the surface of *Tintern Abbey* and the *Prelude*. It also presents more vividly and states more emphatically than the other poems some of the particular points of intersection between sexuality, gender, and social class, and in this respect it stands as a sort of commentary on the subtexts of those poems.[26]

It is now commonly recognized that *Nutting* can be read on one level as a story of rape and that the portrayal of rape includes within it a commentary on the relations between masculine sexuality and imperialist conquest.[27] Nature is feminized, the female body is territorialized, and the masculine adventurer in the poem forces his way into this feminine territory (16), ecstatically destroying its peaceful beauty and out of that destruction making himself "rich beyond the wealth of kings" (51). If in the boat-stealing episode in the *Prelude* the isolated poet learned to respect private property, here he learns the imperialist tactic of appropriating natural resources and beauties for the purpose of making them into private property of his own possession. And though, as in the boat-stealing episode, his activity produces pangs of guilt ("I felt a sense of pain when I beheld / The silent trees" [52–53]), this guilt is best understood not as a sign of doubt about the essential virtue of acquiring private property, even by violent means, but rather (again as in the boat-stealing episode) as a mechanism by which the conversion of nature into private property is injected with human value: guilt does not prevent the sexually charged violation of nature, modify the indiscriminate exercise of extreme violence, or deter the imperialist drive to destroy nature and convert it into private property; rather, it simply appears after the fact as a shaping value upon which are hung the activities that have already been carried out. Guilt humanizes and personalizes the sadistic actions that have transpired, cleansing them of their violent horror and civilizing them without changing them; in this way, guilt assures that sexual violence and imperialist conquest are sanctified.

There are several small details in the poem that bear on its portrayal of masculine identity, sexual violence, and imperialist conquest. First, in the early portion of the poem, the poet's description of his activity preparatory to his excursion helps to identify the class dimension of imperialism. The poet does not embark on his adventure in his own identity but rather dresses down for the occasion, "Tricked out in proud disguise of cast-off weeds / Which for that service had been husbanded, / By exhortation of my frugal Dame" (9–11). In fact, as he admits, he is "More ragged than need was!" (14). After his vicious imperialistic encroachment on a virgin territory "unseen by any human eye" (32), he emerges "rich beyond the wealth of kings," an act that marks a radical transformation of his character from extraordinarily poor to extraordinarily wealthy, thanks to his violent and mutilating conduct.

The distance between the poet's initial (disguised) poverty-ridden condition and his subsequent accumulation of untold wealth can be read in various ways, all of which, however, must acknowledge the masculinist center of the narrative. For example, the development of the narrative may be regarded as a poetic sign of individual fluidity and mobility under the reigning authority of imperialist ideology: even the poorest (male) individuals stand to benefit from the opportunities made available by a politics of imperialist conquest and accumulation. Or the narrative may be seen as a poetic statement about the class dimension of imperialist conquest: the actual violent labor of imperialism is carried out by the poor; the poet's disguise acknowledges this fact, and his subsequent wealth marks the true hands into which imperialist wealth falls—not the poor but rather the bourgeois subject standing behind and over the labors of the poor. Or, again, on a more narrowly psychological level, the poem may be seen as a commentary on the disguise worn by the robber-rapist, who hides behind a mask to pursue his desires for wealth and sexual power and whose secret activity is (always) subsequently chastened and thereby sanctified by his feelings of guilt.

In any reading, however—whether focusing on bourgeois potential, class exploitation, or psychological drive—the masculine subject controls the meanings of the narrative, and he does so at the expense of a violently mutilated feminine object, who is at once an object of (masculine) sexual desire and imperial conquest. The guilt that haunts the narrator, much like the guilt in the boat-stealing episode in the *Prelude*, cannot change the fact of violence that stands at the center of the narrative and in fact serves to reinforce masculine identity by suggesting a virtuous depth that must lie behind violent activity. The final lines of the poem become disturbingly ambiguous in light of this perspective:

> Then, dearest Maiden, move along these shades
> In gentleness of heart; with gentle hand
> Touch—for there is a spirit in the woods. (54–56)

A human female presence is here abruptly introduced into the poem and instructed in the proper relation of the human to nature, the lesson apparently deriving its ideological authority from the violence and guilt that the narrator has just experienced. But even if, on the surface, the lesson is benevolently presented, describing the importance of human gentleness and the presence of spiritual life in nature, at the same time it is haunted by what has gone before—the mutilation of a feminized nature by a masculine-imperialist aggressor. In light of their imperialist, class, and sexist context, in fact, these lines sound not so much like a benevolent lesson as like a masculine threat to a young woman; that is, they sound like a warning to her that she, too, could be mutilated if she does not heed the "spirit in the woods." That spirit, according to the events described in earlier sections of the poem, is emphatically masculine, and its authority is solidified by the clear example of physical violence that stands behind it. While this reading runs directly against the grain of the lines' expressive intention, it nevertheless points to one important level at which textual meaning must be grasped: the "Maiden" here is clearly a corollary of the feminized nature that has earlier been violated, and she is addressed by the same masculine identity that had mutilated nature. Before, that identity was physically abusive and intrusive, and now it is rhetorically forceful and domineering. It has changed only insofar as its authority comes to be expressed at the level of ideology rather than at the level of physical force—but the authority itself has not changed at all, a fact that of course calls attention once more to the vital connection between sadeian logic and romantic idealism.

The final lines of the poem may serve, further, to assure ongoing masculine pleasure in the domination of the feminine. That is, these lines not only may represent ideologically the violence that stands at the heart of the masculinist-imperialist identity; at the same time, they mark a *containment* of violence that assures its repeatable pleasure. The address to the Maiden, as an act of self-restraint that also restrains the object of address, is a calculation of power; it is a measure of the speaker's authority, over both himself and the Maiden, that assures his durable control over the degree, intensity, and frequency of his pleasure. He is violent; he is capable of guilt; he is benevolent: he possesses not only an explicit, surface-bound power but also a human dimension capable of restraining and valuing explicit violence, the combination of which enables him to calculate precisely an object of pleasure that stands within reach of violence and to discover pleasure in the calculation itself—to discover pleasure, that is, in the promise of future and repeatable pleasure. Goux's description of bourgeois libido, cited above, captures the significance of these lines very well: the bourgeois subject postpones jouissance in favor of thriftiness and finds jouissance, instead, in the spare economy of calculation.[28] Postponement and calculation, in turn, enable the bourgeois masculine subject to universalize itself, for they effectively lift masculine subjectivity beyond its grounding violence to a level where it becomes the measure of all value.

The power and importance of a poem like *Nutting* lie in the fact that it places side by side the extremes of bourgeois masculinist authority. The sexual violence that is presented with numbing repetition in the narratives of Sade is presented here in symbolic language alongside a powerful and sincere expression of romantic desire. But they are not shown as mutually exclusive human tendencies; rather, they are shown to be vitally linked as parts of a single masculine identity, which emerges within a historical moment of imperialist expansion and violent conquest. Sadeian logic and romantic idealism may deny the claims of each upon the other, but, as *Nutting* persuasively shows, they are inextricably bound to one another within the rising energies of a newly triumphant world of bourgeois individualism and bourgeois patriarchy.

On the most general level, of course, the patriarchal relations operating in Wordsworth's poetry are not unique to capitalism and a bourgeois world order, insofar as those relations are predicated upon—and are an articulation of—the oppression of women, which preexisted capitalism. But the nature of women's oppression is, emphatically, historically specific, changing form along with the full range of social relations taken over by capitalism: the family, law, religion, education, and so on. One necessary step, therefore, in understanding patriarchy and moving to overcome its oppressive authority is the investigation of its particular historical contours. Such an investigation necessarily involves charting its singular form of logic, which stretches across the entire cultural and social landscape from its most benevolent to its most violent corners, and disclosing the levels of its operation. This means not only establishing the particular formative authority of capitalism over patriarchy but also examining the relations between different expressions of patriarchy—from sadism to romanticism—to locate its most irreducible historical features so that ways of imagining alternative forms of culture and expression can begin.

The project that I am describing here, as my consideration of *Tintern Abbey,* the *Prelude,* and *Nutting* makes clear, assumes that during the romantic period there are close relations between visionary idealism, patriarchy, and sadism. But, as I have suggested, this is not to say that the task of tracing those connections, and of interrogating the oppressive logic of gender in particular romantic texts, should be carried out with the intention of rejecting the romantic project and its more noble aspirations. It should be carried out, rather, with the aim of explaining the social energies motivating those aspirations and, by explaining them, opening them out onto the larger historical landscape of which they are a part. *Tintern Abbey,* for instance, need not be viewed as a dangerous or manipulative poem to recognize that its formulation of gender is connected to the larger, and conflicted, ideological currents of an emergent bourgeois worldview. Quite the reverse, the poem becomes a vitally important historical document insofar as it carries within it a logic and vision of moral possibility and human integrity that are grounded upon specific relations of gender—relations that endorse the private (masculine) appropriation and use of the feminine in the construction of a bourgeois masculine subjectivity. To recognize this logic of gender is to begin to understand the shaping pressure of bourgeois history on Wordsworth's grand imagination.

Chapter Three

Coleridge

Coleridge's poetry provides what is probably the richest territory of critical investigation in the present study because it is both self-consciously imaginative and intellectual. Its self-consciousness brings into the poetry a certain psychological and cultural anxiety, which in turn provides glimpses into the many shades and nuances of gender-significant meaning not as readily accessible in the poetry of Wordsworth and Keats. Coleridge's poetry surpasses that of most of his contemporaries in its profound statement of the complexity, dread, hope, and sheer confusion surrounding questions of gender. The richness of Coleridge's imaginative vision for feminist analysis is evident everywhere in his poetry: in its exploration and articulation of the complex inner workings of fear, in its studied attention to the logical frameworks around which philosophical speculation must be structured, in its portrayal of the limitations and possibilities of language as a source and vehicle for meaning, and in its bold representation of the relations of myth and legend to forms of desire and thought. While his vision often weakens, or occasionally even collapses, under the weight of its own self-consciousness and intellectuality, it nevertheless reveals—even at those moments when it recognizes its own limitations—important dimensions of gender in relation to specifically masculine mental structures. In the following pages, I wish to examine several of Coleridge's poems— *Christabel, The Nightingale, The Eolian Harp*, and *The Rime of the Ancient Mariner*—in an effort to elucidate the central importance of gender to his imaginative vision.

1.

The critical history of *Christabel,* in some respects, looks like a particularly profound playing out of the endless deferral and proliferation of
meanings that much contemporary theory claims to be characteristic of
textuality. To a degree unmatched by the academic study of most other
romantic texts (with the possible exception of the *Rime of the Ancient
Mariner*), criticism of *Christabel* is marked by uncertainty and extremity in its recurrent efforts to sort through and master the insurmount-
able and complicating facts of the poem's fragmentary status, its mystifying representation of Geraldine's bosom and side, the unclear purpose
and dubious integrity of the conclusions of parts one and two, its
composition and publication history, the relations between its romance
and historical elements, Coleridge's claim that he knew exactly how the
poem was supposed to conclude, and his failure to divulge that conclusion. However these particulars may have been negotiated by scholars
and critics at various moments in the past, they have never been satisfactorily settled and have always seemed to stand as visible proof that
the poem cannot be entirely mastered by interpretation. The glaring
difficulty of accounting adequately for the disparate details and ideas
inscribed in and associated with the poem—a difficulty seen even in the
tireless and brilliant efforts to place every last poetic reference within a
single explanatory scheme[1]—throws into relief a difficulty, also fore-
grounded in much contemporary theory, of interpretation itself: the
often majestic but always failed efforts to control and reduce the rich
complexity of *Christabel* suggest in retrospect that the poem does not
constitute an expression of coherent meaning but rather represents a
sort of absence, or vacuum, which pulls critical writing into it to supply
meaning, which the poem itself lacks.[2]

To remark upon the large failure of the critical effort to provide a
coherent and stable explanation of the poem, of course, is not to deny
the particular accomplishment of that effort or to argue that criticism
should stop talking about the ways in which *Christabel* makes meaning
possible. It is rather to say simply what scholars and critics have come
to know in an age informed by poststructuralist thinking: that interpretations tend to be provisional rather than absolute, partial rather than
complete, because they rely upon particular linguistic and textual components that can always be differently arranged and valued. But, as my
initial reference to the critical *history* of the poem suggests, to comment
on the failure of earlier criticism is also to call attention to what critics

have begun to learn (perhaps anew) under the authority of recent historicist thinking: that partial and provisional interpretations are historically contingent, governed not only by the object of critical inquiry (the literary text) but also by the structures of social life that undergird that object and by the forms of authority and belief from which critical activity itself begins. This historical claim is important because it calls our attention to the active human context of literature and its study, refusing some poststructuralist claims that meanings are only textual and linguistic constructions subject to their own deconstruction. As I argued in chapter 1, without denying textuality, the best historicist thought urges the investigation of the conditions—both textual and extratextual, literary and critical—that are necessary to the production of meaning.

The poststructuralist and historicist interventions into the problem of literary meaning have produced at least three lessons on interpretation that are perhaps by now commonplace but that nevertheless can be usefully recalled here as a way of marking out some of the problems and concerns surrounding the critical investigation of *Christabel:* (1) like all historical activity, interpretation necessarily will continue struggling within and against the conditions of its own existence, even as it strives for thoroughness and objectivity in carrying out its investigation of meaning; (2) it ultimately must confront the ineluctable presence and importance, at every level, of textuality, and the repeatable constructions and deconstructions associated with textuality; and (3) most contentiously, it must understand that its activity is always and unavoidably political insofar as it is historically and textually implicated—it is always intricately bound to some implicit or explicit (and historically locatable) interest and cannot carve out an entirely neutral space for itself that stands apart from the various and complex conditions that both enable and limit its activity. Historicist thinking in a poststructuralist age, in other words, forces recognition of the fact that meanings—and the deconstruction of meanings—are always contestable and that their contestability is a mark of their turbulent human location, where power and knowledge are constantly being claimed, negotiated, exchanged, and lost. While in the first instance, perhaps, a textual logic can problematize interpretation and makes deconstruction possible, in the last instance historical conditions determine the specific authority of that logic and thus determine as well the contours, possibilities, and limitations of interpretation.

It is useful, and perhaps necessary, to preface a discussion of *Christabel* with these rather nervous comments not only because they help to indicate my own thinking about critical practice generally but, more importantly, because they point toward the particular critical avenue that I wish to take into the poem. First, the above comments are meant to emphasize an abiding critical assumption of this study, namely that interpretation is still possible and necessary: as long as the meaning of literature is located not only in its own pastness but also in the relation of the present to the past, then interpretation will serve the important function of helping to chart the terrain of that relation. Second, the above comments emphasize once more my view that interpretation constitutes an either implicit or explicit intervention and appropriation of its object of inquiry and thus not only describes preexistent meanings, or helps to crystalize details and ideas from the past, but also registers and shapes assumptions and intellectual perspectives of the present: an interpretation of *Christabel* stakes out as its own a territory of thought and belief having to do not only with the past but also with the cultural context of interpretative practice itself. Finally, these comments acknowledge the imbeddedness of social and political meaning in textuality, an acknowledgment, as I have suggested, that does not give over all meaning to texts but nevertheless recognizes textuality as one necessary site of political practice and critical explanation alike.

In what follows, the above claims provide the bases for critical investigation of certain features of *Christabel* that, I believe, help to elucidate the poem's textual depth and historical richness. I take for granted, as these critical and theoretical remarks might suggest, the contentious nature of my argument; and, as with the discussion of Wordsworth in chapter 2, I pursue a strategy of strong reading, following and appropriating lines of Coleridge's poem in such a way as to raise different sorts of historical questions about its language, the textual and cultural conditions that might shape a reader's view of that language, and the relation of the poem and its underlying assumptions to certain issues important in feminist analysis today. In other words, the act of interpretation that I carry out is a particular *use* of *Christabel* that speaks about the poem in order to speak as well about something beyond the poem.

2.

Christabel is a quintessential romantic poem portraying a benevolent and principled individual who sincerely yearns to overcome loneliness and alienation and to discover a life characterized by stability, fullness, charity, and compassion. It is also marked by a strong gothic sensibility insofar as its expressions of desire are accompanied by severe psychological anxiety and even dread, arising from an encounter with the unknown.[3] While these prominent romantic and gothic elements call attention to certain features of personal life, at the same time they reflect a range of larger concerns having to do with the underlying, and troubled, structures of the difficult physical and social world that the characters of the poem are forced to inhabit. The poem portrays romantic nature in all its beauty and potentially redemptive authority while at the same time revealing the nightmarish possibilities that haunt the edges of nature and perhaps even inhabit its center. It suggests as well the pressure on the romantic imagination generated by profound changes in the class structure of society. Finally, it locates these various ideas and issues in and around the situation of women in society: Christabel and Geraldine seem to represent opposite extremes and possibilities within the disturbed social world of the poem. To explain the operation and relation of these and other similar issues is to provide a preliminary strategy for addressing far-reaching critical and political questions about romanticism that feminist thought today eventually must answer.

One of the most important, and perhaps obvious, facts about the social dimension of *Christabel* is that, notwithstanding the powerful, expressive, and even uplifting romantic imagination that produced the poem, the narrative line rides a declining social energy. From the beginning, the world that Christabel inhabits is weakened and divided against itself. Ostensibly governed by the chivalrous, confident, and definitive authority of the father (1.106–11), defended by a military body under the service of the law (1.127–28), and characterized by cultural codes arising from, and reflecting, stable feudal-aristocratic social conditions (for example, 2.338–44), the world of the poem in fact is hollow, unable to protect or uphold the values that it considers to be sacred. Its inhabitants, in their various ways, loudly proclaim the authority and integrity of their world while at the same time demonstrating in their actions its real diminishing stability.[4] As Michael Cooke has pointed out, the very fact that Christabel, in the beginning of the poem, has left her father's castle in the middle of the night to pray alone in the forest is a sure sign that something is wrong and that Sir Leoline does not possess the absolute authority that appears to belong to him.[5] (It may also be a sign of a sort of protestant religious turn against the public and culturally sanctioned expression of religious devotion associated with Catholicism under the auspices of aristocratic feudalism.)

When this insight is combined with the fact of Sir Leoline's ill health (1.118), the ease with which Geraldine penetrates into the walls and life of the castle, and Sir Leoline's blindness to his patriarchal responsibilities respecting his daughter, it becomes evident that Langland Hall has lost some of its authority over the world it professes to command.

But any recognition of the diminishing world of *Christabel* must be set alongside the poem's clear effort to hold destabilization and decline in check by a strong rhetoric of determination and control. Although Christabel initiates the action that leads to her apparent demise, both by leaving the castle and by physically assisting Geraldine into the castle, she is, at least in part 1, entirely confident of her father's authority and of the stability of her world. And although, in part 2, Sir Leoline seems determined to make every move that will jeopardize his daughter and threaten his own well-being, he is unwaveringly confident of his ability to assist Geraldine, atone for the sins of his past, and effect a renewed personal and social life of solidarity, compassion, and friendship. While these instances of Sir Leoline's confidence are offset by Bard Bracy's vocal anxiety and Geraldine's apparent demonic nature, they nevertheless register a ruling-class aristocratic sensibility of coherent authority, a sensibility out of tune with the realities of the world, to be sure, but one that emphatically displays the attitudes and values that once ruled absolutely and that Sir Leoline and Christabel believe continue to rule, despite their own actions that contradict that belief.

The tension between the fact of social decline and the assumption of stable authority is responsible for some of the poem's thematic complexities and formal ambiguities. While the important individuals inhabiting Christabel's world, along with the expressed values of that world, are emphatically aristocratic—Sir Leoline, Lord Roland de Vaux, the lady "so richly clad" (1.67)—practical life in the narrative does not always follow aristocratic cultural codes and social expectations. Christabel's secret conduct is nothing less than a transgression against aristocratic patriarchal law; Geraldine appears to manipulate and undermine aristocratic and patriarchal authority to satisfy her own personal ends; even Sir Leoline, in his conduct toward his daughter, violates the codes that he himself has explicitly set forth and would embody.

This particular portrayal of social contradiction, however, is not a picture of the sort of personal, or bourgeois, alienation and anxiety that will characterize, say, the Victorian novel, in which characters are divided souls, cast out from a world they detest; rather it is a picture of internal social decay, in which personal and public values are identical, but neither the individual nor society is able any longer to live out these values to which both are committed. The various characters—with the possible exception of Geraldine—follow a line of conduct that is radically incommensurate with the public values they themselves articulate and want to embrace, and in doing so they show that they are not so much divided against their social world as faced with a social reality that is no longer able to sustain them because it can no longer sustain itself. And this problematic *social* situation renders extraordinarily complex the relation of individuals to one another, to the society whose authority they vocally support, and to the values and principles that seem in fact to motivate their personal lives.

In an argument against reducing the narrative to a narrowly psychological explanation, the question necessarily arises, on a purely practical-critical level, how to assess the poem's portrayal of Christabel's loss of innocence; the ignorant good intentions of Sir Leoline; the apparently malevolent aims of Geraldine; the prophetic but powerless insights of Bard Bracy; the narrator's romanticized notions of a transhistorical benevolent authority; the near-obsession, by some of the characters and by the narrator, with Christabel's absent mother.[6] Partly because of the fragmentary nature of the narrative, but also partly because of the very social instability that I am foregrounding, these and other matters become impossible to reduce to a single explanation; at best, they can be seen as signs of loss, as traces of—or nostalgic longing for—a once noble, secure, and rich social authority that now exists only at the level of memory, rhetoric, and desire. One result, narratively, of the claim for social stability within a context of declining social authority, or declining coherence of social vision, is that thematic unity is shredded, characters' actions are inconsistent and self-contradictory, and various discrete thematic interests follow the conflicted course of a deracinated social structure of authority, belief, and value.

The formal character of *Christabel* is similarly complicated by the clash between individual action and structures of social authority articulated in the narrative. Indeed, one may argue that the poem's fragmentary status is, at least in part, a result of an incoherent social vision rather than the other way around. It is unlikely that the various threads of action, or the characterizations and conflicting controlling ideas, could ever be pulled together into any real vision of organic unity representative of the sort of romantic visionary idealism to which the poem appears committed at the level of expressive intention.

But there are other formal difficulties as well that have been re-marked in several excellent discussions of the poem.[7] The numerous and often awkward intrusions by the narrative voice; the apparent stabs at humor that are offset by gothic horror or melodrama; the placement of conclusions to the first and second parts in an apparent attempt to control the meaning of what has gone before (much as the marginal gloss seems designed to control the meanings of the *Rime of the Ancient Mariner*)—these suggest a narrative anxiety born of an uncertainty about how to keep together the numerous interests and problems of the plot. At one moment the poem seems prepared to laugh at itself, to foreground its own linguistic gamesmanship, and to turn the narrative into a sort of self-deconstructive joke, while at another it seems pre-pared to be genuinely horrified at the events it attempts to represent; and at still other moments it seems entirely confident of its own integrity and thematic purpose.[8] The narrator, moreover, occasionally fades into the intricate textures of the narrative, only to reemerge, almost without warning, as a voice not unlike Byron's narrator in *Don Juan,* yabbering on about his characters in a way suggesting his inability to control their fates ("O shield her! shield sweet Christabel!" [1.254]) and lamenting their various hardships and actions. Formally as well as thematically, the poem refuses to be mastered, producing textual signs of its own confusion that at the same time carry within them a rich complexity born of ambiguous (and ever multiplying) relations between intellection and ideological aspiration on the one hand and textual and social instability on the other.

If the poem, as I am suggesting, signifies both social and textual breakdown, at the same time it registers in important ways the complex social and ideological parameters and dimensions of that breakdown and thereby—even against its own expressive intention—discovers its particular aesthetic possibilities and integrity. For the negative energy that the narrative line follows is not transparent or weak but richly laden with the public and personal meanings caught in the structural transformation of society that is registered in the poem, and it carries within it at least the seeds of its dialectical opposite. That is, even as the poem thematizes personal contradiction and social decline, it discloses certain inchoate, deep-seated, and complex historical energies and so-cial relations beginning to take form as a determining authority over the structures of personal and social life defining the aristocratic worldview of Christabel and Sir Leoline.

The rich complexity of the poem's social energy can be glimpsed by expanding Karen Swann's useful insight that Sir Leoline's law is at the center of the poem.[9] That law is the definitive expression of human reason and the anchor of social order, and it is essentially masculine in nature, assuming that the absolute rule of the father not only secures public life generally but also assigns identity and value to women. The law upheld by Sir Leoline is openly accepted by Christabel and Bracy alike and is respected, apparently, even by Geraldine. But, as I have suggested, events in the narrative demonstrate that Sir Leoline's law is severely weakened, as the actions of Christabel, Geraldine, and Sir Leoline himself are incommensurate with its expectations. And in its weakened condition, it is challenged and disrupted even as, at the level of rhetoric, it appears to hold turmoil and difference in check.

Virtually every action presented in the narrative shows the emergence of a way of perceiving and valuing the world that is radically different from what Sir Leoline's law commands. The actions, mentioned above, of Christabel, Geraldine, and Sir Leoline himself, in their various ways, mark an effort to reconstitute human relations along more personal, or subjective, lines than allowed by Sir Leoline's authority. When Christabel secretly leaves the castle to pray "For the weal of her lover that's far away" (1.30), she follows an independent course of action that ultimately, and irrevocably, opens the way for the thorough subversion of the law of the father. Further, however subservient Geraldine appears to be to the wishes and commands of Sir Leoline, in fact she follows a design of her own making over which Sir Leoline has no authority and to which, in fact, he becomes entirely subservient. And when Sir Leoline himself eagerly sets about assisting Geraldine, he actively violates the responsibilities of his position in favor of his nostalgic desire to recover certain deeply personal relations of his past.

The social disruption that these characters' actions point to, in other words, carries within it an elementary but sure oppositional sensibility, one certainly not well defined in the narrative but grounded nonetheless in a fairly firm commitment to personal or subjective—or bourgeois— desire imposed on the feudal-aristocratic world of the poem from Coleridge's position in the late eighteenth century. The law of the father associated with Sir Leoline's name does indeed represent the central authority of Christabel's world, but it is also opposed in the narrative by a diffuse set of rising energies that appear to run the gamut from spiritually benevolent to threateningly demonic. Any explanation of gender relations in the poem must account for the force of these energies against the feudal-aristocratic authority represented in the character of Sir Leoline.

Only Bracy the bard appears to be exempt from the contradictions that I am associating with the other characters; thus, before examining the relations of those contradictions to the portrayal of gender, I want to pause here long enough to consider his place in the narrative. Bracy is interesting not only because he appears to hold more firmly than the other characters to the codes and customs associated with Sir Leoline's law but also because he is an artist in the service of the feudal estate. His character is distinguished by its firm sense of a unified and meaningful ideal that corresponds unproblematically to the aristocratic authority governing the state, the individual, and nature.

One way of understanding Bracy's importance to the poem's social vision—and to its textual complexity—is to consider that the meanings associated with his idealizing perspective anticipate Coleridge's theory of the symbol, presented in *The Statesman's Manual,* which holds that "a symbol . . . is characterized by . . . the translucence of the Eternal through and in the Temporal . . . ; and while it enunciates the whole, abides itself as a living part in that Unity, of which it is the representative."[10] When this view is translated into a poetic narrative about individuals, institutions, and values—as Coleridge intended it to be—it becomes remarkably descriptive of Bracy's understanding of the relations between the everyday world in which he lives and works and the ideals that he articulates. His responsibility, as he understands it, is not simply to celebrate the authority of Sir Leoline but also to clear away or absorb the contradictions that may stand between individuals and the state on one hand and a higher, benevolent, and determining authority on the other. Like the poet of *Kubla Khan,* his is a difficult labor, one requiring that "With music strong and saintly song / . . . [He] wander through the forest bare, / Lest aught unholy loiter there" (2.561–63)— that is, requiring that he prepare the natural ground for a proper and redemptive relation between the temporal and eternal, and represent the unity (ideally) constituted in this relation.

What is perhaps most remarkable about Bracy is that, despite his role as the artistic voice of aristocratic and patriarchal authority, and despite his recognition of the severity of the social situation before him, he is utterly unable to carry out the artistic-social responsibility with which his character is identified. He is apparently exempt from the contradictions that define the other characters, and he is clearly identified as someone of integrity and nobility of intention, and yet his abilities are absolutely defeated when he is thrown against his will into the social morass from which he would save Sir Leoline and pressed to serve the very forces that he would oppose. Thus his own character and actions are made to produce the opposite of what he himself holds up as truth. He is a perfect example of the ineffectual romantic artist, who recognizes the potential for beauty and the saving authority of eternal truth but is hit so hard by social circumstance that he is unable to express that recognition clearly or to bring ideal beauty and truth into the world: he sees beyond the contradictions that entrap his fellow citizens and yet is finally unable to escape them and is thus not only rendered helpless but also pressed to destroy the very ideals that he articulates.

This view of Bracy's socially ensnared idealism becomes important not simply because it is consistent with a pattern of thought discernible in much of Coleridge's work but also because it helps to focus the encroaching secularization of social life in the world of the poem. According to the narrative, the spiritual ideals that once provided social coherence are now rejected, and what is left is the pressing reality of historical change, with its many hardships, struggles, and desperate hopes. Bracy's inability to alter, transcend, or accommodate historical change or social circumstance, along with the portrayal of Geraldine in demonic terms, casts a pall over the narrative, suggesting the loss of spirituality, the inability of artistic vision to recall it, and the probable demise of human life into a social quagmire of difficulty and deceit.

But this apparent downward spiral of human life into the depths of historical and social necessity does not represent the limit of the poem's vision. At the same time that it portrays spiritual loss, the narrative also encourages, tentatively or vaguely, a rereading of social life from the point of view of society itself. The marginalization of Bracy, and the decentering of spiritual life that is entailed in that marginalization, force a reconsideration of the dimensions and possibilities of the world being opened up by Geraldine. While that world appears dangerous and demonic to Bracy and Christabel—and probably to Coleridge—it nonetheless can be seen to constitute a radical reconceptualization of society that cannot be avoided and that in fact brings its own unique views to bear on human need and desire.

3.

The relation between these various social matters and the poem's particular formulation of gender is problematic at best because every character and situation is caught amid social and historical crosscurrents, and within personal traumas, that complicate masculine and feminine identity. Christabel, for instance, is clearly drawn in sympathetic terms, as a Christlike individual motivated by compassion, charity, goodwill, and loyalty to her father and family; and yet her actions early in the narrative are patently transgressive and call into play the disruptive events that become her fate.[11] Whatever one may wish to say about the personal appeal and integrity of Christabel's character, the moment of her transgression is definitive, opening up her relation to turbulent social and sexual energies and pointing not only outward to the difficult world in which she lives but also back onto the most private dimensions of her character, spelling her sure and absolute entanglement in circumstances radically different from her expectations of personal and social life.

Such narrative twists make it difficult to disentangle entirely the wrenching crosscurrents and traumas that mark Christabel in gender-specific ways. And it is similarly difficult to specify other characters—as well as the various personal and public situations and ideas inscribed in the narrative—in such a way as to identify precisely the operations of gender in the poem. Nevertheless, I believe that it is possible to construct some of the contexts within which gender emerges in the narrative and to speculate on the probable intersections between gender and social transformation.

One important means of getting at the poem's formulation of gender is to recognize the necessary relation between the contradictions of Sir Leoline's world and the contradictions of Christabel's character. The rhetoric of authority offset by the reality of weakness and ill-health that identifies Sir Leoline finds its corollary in Christabel's vocal acceptance of father-law, which is offset by the centering of her actions around subjective determination. Christabel, in other words, is both a model daughter of patriarchy and an agent of its disruption. Whatever her personal intentions may be with respect to the wishes of her father— and she later proves duly submissive to those wishes—her conduct exemplifies at least an inchoate feminine subjectivity and assertiveness that take advantage of her father's weakening authority in an effort to further her own desires. Put somewhat differently, her secret venture into the forest outside the castle begins from the weakening social controls of the father and then unleashes new (feminine) energies (in the form of Geraldine) that take further advantage of that weakness. Christabel's personal desire is therefore (although unbeknownst to her) also social in the beginning, and it proceeds relentlessly along social lines—even after personal desire has diminished—against the grain of her father's authority.

But while the social weakness emblematized in Sir Leoline's ill health (and even in the events listed in Bard Bracy's dream) provides an opportunity for feminine agency, crisis and transformation do not present themselves neatly as a one-directional movement. Christabel *is* a daughter under the authority of feudal-aristocratic patriarchy, and whatever encourages her early actions or informs subsequent events, the authority of that patriarchy remains quite real and (as the latter portion of the narrative shows) even threatening. This fact is plainly seen in the very act of Christabel's transgression, for, while she is motivated by personal desire, that desire is not entirely hers; at the very least, the form of her desire derives from the rule of the father.

Christabel's desire, exemplified in her secret prayer for her betrothed, is invested in the man who will take over from her father the role of protector. Her desire never reaches beyond the realm of heterosexual masculine authority, remaining entirely contained within the parameters of patriarchy. The degree of her dependence on the rule of the father, even when she stands literally outside the bounds of its authority (that is, in the forest), is seen as well in her expressed certainty that her father will protect Geraldine and restore the distressed maiden to the hands of her own father:

> O well, bright dame! may you command
> The service of Sir Leoline;
> And gladly our stout chivalry
> Will he send forth and friends withal
> To guide and guard you safe and free
> Home to your noble father's hall. (1.106–11)

Christabel's desire is both real and feminine, but it is circumscribed in determining ways by the social reality of feudal-aristocratic patriarchy, and it cannot manifest itself except in ways that would entail its recontainment by the very authority that it would escape. At best, therefore, her transgression must be read as a desire for desire, as it expresses at once feminine courage and masculine control.

The extent of masculine control over (Christabel's) feminine desire— and the skewed nature of feminine desire under the control of feudal patriarchy—is glimpsed in part 2 of the narrative when Sir Leoline meets Geraldine. Here, Sir Leoline becomes so infatuated with the beautiful Geraldine, and so enamored of his own memories of the past, that he utterly ignores his own daughter, even to the point of feeling betrayed by her when she fails to express the same happiness that he feels:

> His heart was cleft with pain and rage,
> His cheeks they quivered, his eyes were wild,
> Dishonoured thus in his old age;
> Dishonoured by his only child. (2.640–43)

Christabel's genuine hopes earlier in the narrative and her certainty about her father's benevolence and chivalry are dashed as Sir Leoline shows himself to be blind to and helpless before the dangers that lie directly in front of him and violently angry at those who would expose those dangers. What began, for Christabel, as desire formulated within patriarchal limits, and as loyalty to the values contained within those limits, becomes a depressing recognition of the hopeless fate of the narrow vision of aristocratic patriarchy, in which chivalry and a romanticized past take precedence over any claims put forth by even the most well-intentioned daughters.

If Christabel unleashes the forces and energies that threaten to destroy the already weakening structures of Sir Leoline's world, Geraldine is the complicated figure who embodies those forces and energies.[12] Like Christabel, she is a woman who carries a deep-seated desire within her; but unlike Christabel, she does not begin from within the walls of patriarchal authority, and for this reason her desire is more adamantly feminine and threatening: it is uncontrolled by the assumptions and goals that limit Christabel's desire. While the threat she represents is most often read—and indeed the narrative itself apparently would have readers so view her character—in demonic terms, it is possible to understand her demonism not as essential to her character but rather as a sign of her *relation* to aristocratic and patriarchal authority.

At every turn, Geraldine refuses the authority and value of aristocratic patriarchy, using these, rather, to serve her own ends; and in that use lies her threatening power. While she appears to be yet another daughter of aristocratic patriarchy, in fact when her physical body is exposed, she seems to represent an explicit refusal of the values that patriarchy would attach to her. While she appears helpless and lost, in fact she is aggressive, securing her strength through her active intervention in the lives of others. While she possesses beauty capable of winning the attentions of men, she takes her sexual strength from the embrace of another woman rather than from men. She is demonic, in short, insofar as she denies, challenges, and subverts the most sacred codes and authority of a world that Christabel attempts to resist but within which she remains entrapped.

Geraldine's curious power might be seen as an extreme representation of the desire that Christabel desires but lacks the courage to follow. Geraldine is the energy, born of Christabel's surreptitious adventure in the forest, that forces recognition of the contradictions in aristocratic patriarchy that Christabel, while momentarily emboldened by those contradictions, ultimately would seal over. She is a positive assault on an apparently monolithic social and ideological structure of authority that has secured entirely for itself the vocabulary of spiritual honor and integrity, leaving Geraldine's energy and character only the vocabulary and conduct of the demon, which she embraces and carries forward with great effect.[13]

But, like Christabel, Geraldine is not a transparent character. She is both agent and victim, reluctantly following an energy whose direction and character she seems at times to doubt. She does not relish her penetration of Sir Leoline's castle or her seduction of Christabel. In some respects she appears to be the genuinely helpless individual whom Christabel meets in the beginning of the narrative, driven along, like Coleridge's Mariner, by forces beyond her control—she "eyes the maid and seeks delay" (1.259)—to effect a disruption, and subversion, of accepted sexual conduct, religious belief, family stability, and chivalrous codes. Almost against her will she embodies and carries to an extreme the contradictions reflected in the characters of Christabel and Sir Leoline, and she opens those contradictions out to such an extent that they can never be resolved, or recontained, by the feudal and patriarchal structures of social life out of which they are born.[14] She is, as it were, a bearer of historical energy, or desire, that ultimately possesses determining authority over individual identity and agency.

The problematic significance of Christabel's and Geraldine's characters is complicated further by the numerous references in part 1 to Christabel's mother. As the tension between Christabel and Geraldine grows, Christabel at one point laments, "O mother dear! that thou were here!" (1.202), and Geraldine responds, "I would . . . she were" (1.203), and then follows this statement almost immediately by warning Christabel's mother away: "Off, wandering mother! Peak and pine! / I have power to bid thee flee" (1.205–6). In the conclusion to part 1, too, the narrator describes Geraldine's encounter with Christabel in mother-daughter terms, remarking that Geraldine, who "holds the maiden in her arms, / Seems to slumber still and mild, / As a mother with her child" (1.299–301). These repeated calls and references to Christabel's mother, who is loved equally by Christabel and her father, may be read variously as both a desire for and rejection of a conventional maternal presence capable of nurturing and protecting a helpless daughter, as well as an expression of feminine *desire* for a feminine authority. The mother is both desired and rejected and is both absent and, in the form of Geraldine, present; Christabel idealizes her biological mother but is physically drawn into the magical spell cast by Geraldine, becoming a sharer, albeit partly an innocent one, of that woman's energy and activity. To put the matter in slightly different terms, Christabel admires and loves the idea and memory of her mother, but she is drawn into the transgressive physical presence of Geraldine; and Geraldine admires the virtue associated with the memory of Christabel's mother but rejects the powerless role of the biological mother. (Indeed, the death of Christabel's mother in childbirth may be read as an explicit example of female powerlessness, under aristocratic patriarchy, even at a moment expressing great generative power.)

The difficulty, then, is that Christabel's mother is a valued memory but is humanly powerless, and this apparent contradiction may underlie Geraldine's construction of herself as a mother with power—in bed with Christabel, she is like "a mother with her child"—and Christabel's transformation in the narrative from an innocent maiden into a physical woman responsive to sexual embrace. Neither Geraldine nor Christabel responds confidently to the events in which they participate, but the actions of both seem to suggest the desire and perhaps even necessity—insofar as Christabel is utterly unable to alter the situation in which she finds herself—of discovering a feminine power that might move against the current of the authority and expectations of aristocratic patriarchy.

Christabel's expressed desire for the protection of her mother, her confidence in the power of her father, and her plea with her father in part 2 to send Geraldine away need not contradict the line of argument that I am following here. For what must be recognized is that her ideals, fond memories, and virtuous intentions are radically incommensurate with her physical actions, particularly her secret excursion into the forest and her sexual embrace of Geraldine.[15] The excursion into the forest, as I have argued, marks a contradiction, or a weakness, in the world governed by Sir Leoline, and Christabel's actions exploit that contradiction in ways that support the emergence of a threatening alternative authority. Furthermore, they do this despite the nostalgic memories and virtuous expressions of charity, pity, and love that would seem to resist the physical reality of a character such as Geraldine. Christabel's body, one might say, triumphs emphatically over her mind, and that triumph threatens to topple an already weakened patriarchal authority to which she nostalgically clings.

In portraying the various dimensions of feminine desire within the declining structures of aristocratic patriarchy and suggesting the emergence of a more private desire in the characters of Christabel and Geraldine, the poem offers an interesting commentary on the female body. Toward the end of part 1, the narrative takes an eager interest in women disrobing. Once in Christabel's chamber, Geraldine expresses her noble intentions toward Christabel ("for the good which me befel, / Even I in my degree will try, / Fair maiden, to requite you well" [1.230–32]), and then instructs her to "unrobe yourself" (1.233). The description of Christabel's response carries a slight but certain sexual interest: "And as the lady bade, did she. / Her gentle limbs did she undress, / And lay down in her loveliness" (1.236–38). From her bed, as I have suggested, Christabel observes Geraldine, who apparently prays and undresses at the same time, and in such a way that makes her prayer seem less like spiritual expression than sexual enticement:

> Beneath the lamp the lady bowed,
> And slowly rolled her eyes around;
> Then drawing in her breath aloud,
> Like one that shuddered, she unbound
> The cincture from beneath her breast;
> Her silken robe, and inner vest,
> Dropt to her feet. (1.245–51)

What follows is the famous description of Geraldine's mysterious bosom and side and her embrace of the apparently helpless Christabel, both of which encourage a reading of this scene as a sexual encounter punctuated by intense and fearful anxiety over the severity of the physical transgression being committed.

The attention given to disrobing, beyond providing the narrative with a slightly erotic twist, suggests that the female body is approved and adored (as the description of the naked Christabel shows) while at the same time it is resisted and condemned (as the description of the sexually charged Geraldine shows). One possible reason for this apparent contradiction is that Christabel's naked body shows little sign of sexual energy and no sign of sexual autonomy—it is entirely receptive to power being imposed on it—while Geraldine's body teems with sexual energy that follows a path of certain self-gratification that is found not in submission but rather in autonomy, aggressiveness, and control. The exposed bodies of the two women, in other words, explicitly portray the aristocratic patriarchal ideas of good and evil that are under the threat of being confused, or dissolved, in a single sexual embrace generated entirely within a frame of feminine sexuality.

The picture of disrobing also may be read as a shedding of the cultural codes that assign value to women, enabling a material, or physical, groundwork for the construction of a uniquely feminine vision of sexuality, culture, and society. This is perhaps an unduly strong statement, given the fact that throughout part 2 Christabel laments the power that Geraldine has gained over her and is in the process of gaining over her father; but it should be remembered that, as I have shown, part of the complexity of Christabel's character is that it is marked by the various contradictions of her world, so that she can at once express the values and desires of the patriarchal authority associated with her father while at the same time helping to produce the conditions that undermine that authority. Her comments on Geraldine and Sir Leoline need not be taken as transparent, or unproblematic, descriptions of the power dynamics of her world.

Certainly when she and Geraldine disrobe near the end of part 1 they are, if only momentarily, out from under the cultural baggage that each has brought into the bedchamber, and in their denuded condition may represent a desire, however tentative or anxious, entirely ungoverned by the vocabulary and codes upon which both women had relied in the forest and during their return to the castle. That Geraldine becomes "lord of thy utterance" (1.268) when the naked women embrace is a sure sign that Christabel can nevermore submit easily to her father's authority, which until now she had always accepted—even as she resisted—as her fate. From this moment, the weakened authority of Sir Leoline finds an aggressive and sure challenger in the physical assertion of feminine sexuality. In this view, in their disrobing, the women are not weakened but empowered by their own energy and desire.

4.

I want now to recast some of the above issues in terms of the vocabulary of sadism, not so much to focus details of sexual violence in the narrative as to present more specifically the logic of power that I believe governs gender in Christabel's world. There are, of course, touches of violence in the poem that carry with them a sexual interest, as seen, for instance, in Geraldine's narrative of her abduction. According to her,

> Five warriors seized me yestermorn,
> Me, even me, a maid forlorn:
> They choked my cries with force and fright,
> And tied me on a palfrey white.
> . . . .
> I have no thought what men they be. (1.81–84, 90)

Following as it does upon the narrator's sexually tempting descriptions of Geraldine's body ("The neck that made that white robe wan, / Her stately neck, and arms were bare; / Her blue-veined feet unsandal'd were" [1.61–63]), Geraldine's tale of the crime against her carries within it at least a suggestion of a masculine sexual pleasure purchased at the expense of a woman's physical independence and well-being; in this respect her story may be said to follow the typical direction of Sade's narratives of sexual pleasure. Christabel herself, moreover, on one level might be said to resemble Sade's Justine insofar as she is motivated by innocent virtue, which quickly gets her into serious trouble, making her the sexual victim of a deceptive individual whom she would help through a time of trouble.[16]

But such instances of violence and pain and pleasure, while important, do not constitute the core of the poem's sadeian dimension, just as pornographic narratives of sexual violence do not constitute the core of Sade's vision. Rather, the lesson of Sade that helps to illuminate the gender dimension of *Christabel* involves, first, what Annie Le Brun calls "the reality of bodies" and "the intolerable deceitfulness of ideas without bodies."[17] Further, it involves a larger social interest as well; as Jane Gallop remarks, Sade's pornographic work exposes "an institutional structure that is usually covered over."[18] These comments locate sadeian thought at the intersection of the body, the mind, and society, and that intersection is portrayed in such a way as to desanctify "the idea of any community"[19] and to emphasize the particular arrangement of bodies within the desanctified—or fully secularized—community. As Le Brun argues, Sade decenters the human subject, replacing it with a notion of absolute desire that stands categorically on its own, seeking its freedom even at the expense of the human identity through whom it may be expressed.[20] On this account, Sade's narratives are repulsive to most readers not only because of their graphic descriptions of intense sexual cruelty but also because they articulate an entire (gender-based) system of values, beliefs, and assumptions that challenge a conventional humanist understanding of the nature and meaning of human life. What makes this vision so gripping and historically important, even when it may repulse, is that it appears to arise from an absolute and unbending logic, which is given the weight of truth in the sadeian text by its association with repeated acts of excruciating and shocking violence.

As I have argued in previous chapters, this logic often energizes the romantic imagination as well as the sadeian text, though in romanticism its grounding assumptions about gender are usually hidden behind poetic expressions of hope, nostalgia, or benevolent desire. In other words, romantic visionary idealism sometimes covers over the logic of gender—which is, at bottom, a sadeian logic—upon which it often depends for its coherent expression. In obscuring, or even burying, its enabling logic, romanticism effectively evades an important dimension of its historical and cultural construction, one involving ideological violence against women. Any credible effort to defend and extend the claims of the romantic imagination must address this difficult fact.

In light of these observations, it may be useful to attempt a more thoroughgoing materialist analysis of gender in *Christabel* than I have yet offered, one that begins by asking about the particular arrangement of physical bodies in the poem and that considers the relation of individual and social ideas to that arrangement.[21] While, as the title suggests, the poem revolves around Christabel, she is throughout a marginalized figure insofar as she is, in the beginning, compelled to circumvent her father's authority by surreptitiously entering the forest to pray for her absent betrothed and, in part 2, ignored by her father, who turns his attentions wholly to Geraldine. Between these two scenes, she ostensibly controls her own conduct when she assists Geraldine, but in fact she finds herself yet again the object of another's control when, in her own bedchamber, she follows precisely the instructions of Geraldine and receives that woman's (apparently) sexual advances. Her relation to Bracy appears to be more promising insofar as the bard expresses sincere concern for her well-being, but even here she is portrayed as helpless and in need of a male protector.

In the forest, in her bedchamber, and in the Baron's presence-room, Christabel, in her actions and ideas, occupies a subordinate position, standing physically and emotionally to the side of individuals whose authority places them at the center of the various scenes in which they are presented. Her position, in turn, makes possible, and feeds, the claims and desires of Sir Leoline, Geraldine, and even Bracy, whose poetic voice is enlivened by his desire to protect the apparently helpless Christabel. Perhaps the clearest indication of how authority is connected to this positioning and movement of characters is Geraldine, whose movement from one place to another in the narrative duplicates Christabel's. Her movement, however, is not associated consistently with helplessness but, quite the reverse, with increasing power. And it is made very clear that her power comes directly at the expense of Christabel, who weakens precisely to the extent that her counterpart strengthens. This particular formulation of the power dynamic between Geraldine and Christabel reflects perfectly the logic of sadism, which might be said to begin from a zero-sum theory of power and pleasure: because power and pleasure are finite, they can come to one individual only at the expense of another; therefore, Geraldine's increased power *necessitates* Christabel's growing weakness, and Geraldine's pleasure necessitates Christabel's sadness or pain.[22]

But a zero-sum notion of power and pleasure is only one dimension of sadeian logic. Another is the absolute claim of bodies on ideas, and in this claim may be found a liberating possibility—even in the midst of corruption—at least as it is manifested within the narrative of *Christabel*. The physical marginalization of Christabel finds a corollary in her ambiguous relation to ideas, particularly those of her father. But her encounter with Geraldine, while it too is ambiguous in certain ways, constitutes a particular challenge to and disavowal of both those ideas and the structures of social authority they uphold. Geraldine's demonic manipulation of and sexual power over Christabel, in fact, may be said to mark the claim of the female body against a centralized masculinity and masculine definitions of the female body.

With their sexual encounter, Geraldine becomes a dominant female, leading a reluctant Christabel into the inner halls of masculine power and apparently setting up a strategy that will decenter that power and clear a path for an ascendant feminine identity. In this view, the pain that Christabel suffers at the hands of Geraldine is qualitatively different from her subordination to her father and even to Bracy (and different from the pain that Geraldine suffers at the hands of her abductors), for it is a pain that arises from listening to the pleasures of her own body—signaled first not by her sexual encounter with Geraldine but by her secret excursion into the forest—rather than to the authority of her father. If the sadeian vision carries within it a liberating possibility, it is in this recognition of the absolute reality of bodies—the reality of both their capacity for pleasure and pain and their powerful and potentially disruptive claim on ideas, in this case the patriarchal ideas of Sir Leoline. While a zero-sum notion of pleasure and power must ultimately be put into question, here, at least, it is a notion that, when connected to the absolute claims of the body, carries within it the potential of depleting, or dissipating, the social authority of the father over the daughter and regrounding feminine identity in a liberating politics of the body.

I am aware that my assertions here are predicated upon a certain, and contentious, assumption about the redeeming character of Geraldine's actions—and of Sade's thought.[23] But my point is to de-sanctify the community (as Sade might) within which Christabel and her father exist, not to celebrate Geraldine's treatment of Christabel but rather in an effort to get a clearer view of the actual power dynamics that govern that community. One fact that becomes apparent in this desanctifying maneuver is that Geraldine's actions are assigned a nega-tive value primarily within the frame of a masculine, or patriarchal, reality, a reality, as I have argued, that Christabel at once rejects and accepts, detests and desires, but is powerless to disavow entirely with-out the physical intervention of Geraldine.

My claim for Geraldine, therefore, is not a moral one but a political one. While she overwhelms Christabel in ways perhaps no less severe than Sir Leoline's, she does so in a way that begins from the female body, from which is generated an energy that calls into question, absolutely, the claims of men on that body as well as the social claims of aristocratic patriarchy on women. It is likely that the anxiety, humor, and protective interventions ("O shield her! shield sweet Christabel!" [1.254]) associated with the narrative voice of the poem arise, at least partly, from the uncertainty generated by the physical Geraldine, whose mysterious, sensuous, and sexually complex presence cannot be mas-tered by ideas.

Another way of stating the issue that I am trying to describe is to say that the patriarchy of the poem is grounded in a division of the body from the mind. As Jane Gallop remarks in a different context, "men have their masculine identity to gain by being estranged from their bodies and dominating the bodies of others."[24] As I have shown, the authority associated with Sir Leoline is the authority of "custom and law" (2.338), and, while these are ideas, they make claims on bodies, especially (as the portrayal of Christabel illustrates) on the placement and function of female bodies within the patriarchal community, and at the same time they cover over those claims with a rhetoric of trans-historical truth, goodwill, and personal and cultural durability. The role of the mind, or ideas, in the form of law and custom is one reason that disrobing is so important in the poem. The detailed attention to Christabel and Geraldine in a condition of undress, even while it helps to create a masculine erotic interest among romantic and modern audiences, at the same time helps to locate both the object of masculine authority and the necessary (libidinous) source of resistance to that authority—it enables, that is, a reclaiming of the female body.

5.

There remains to be considered, briefly, the relation between the various sociohistorical issues and gender issues that I have been tracing. I have tried to suggest that the narrative portrays a moment of weakening aristocratic patriarchal authority and the emergence of a feminine, or feminist, challenge to that authority in the form of Geraldine. But it is important to understand that that challenge does not constitute an unproblematic liberatory gesture; it stands, rather, as a feminine resistance that remains socially and historically situated, and in ways that must be questioned.

Simply put, the sadeian assertion of the body against the claims of the mind does not constitute a universal truth but rather a historical moment. While the claim of the body is objectively real, it does not escape the mediations of its particular context. In the case of *Christabel*, the assertion of the body occurs both within the gaps opened up by a weakening aristocratic authority and upon the energies generated out of an emergent bourgeois worldview. Christabel's initial transgressive activities are conducted within a sphere of private desire; while that desire is at least partly feudal and aristocratic in definition, at the same time it resists the authority of the aristocratic father and follows a path cut through a landscape of subjectivity and personal life. While they are covered over, as subjectivity and personal life often are, with nostalgic yearning for a public situation, or time, that is coherent, cohesive, and beyond the need for transgressive individual action, their clear presence in Christabel's actions nevertheless marks the desire of the private individual for autonomous identity. Christabel's desires receive their fullest political expression in Geraldine, who appropriates them and manipulates them in a way that enables her intervention into the world of declining aristocratic patriarchy. Together, these women may be said to embody and enact an inchoate bourgeois sensibility, characterized by personal desire and individual action that are identified in opposition to state and cultural authority, as represented by Sir Leoline.

The particular form that this bourgeois sensibility takes may be explained in part as the coalescing of disparate elements that aristocratic patriarchy has cast off or marginalized—the body, personal desire, autonomous individual activity, personal identity—and as the seemingly demonic emergence of these elements from within the energies spilling out from the deterioration of Sir Leoline's authority. It is a sensibility that carries within it residual elements of the world that it would supplant; and it is a sensibility that is implicated, often in brutally negative ways, in the social contradictions that give it life. While Christabel's excursion into the forest can be explained in ways that render her guiltless, it is difficult to read Geraldine's character purely as a positive portrayal of bourgeois energy and vision. In an important respect, a plot-level reading of her character is accurate: she *is* demonic; she *does* deceive, overwhelm, and abuse Christabel; she probably intends to destroy those with whom she comes in contact for the sole purpose of increasing her personal and frightening authority. But to say this is not to offer a moral judgment against her; it is, again, to make a political comment about the problematic and often destructive dimensions of the sensibility that, during the late eighteenth century—that is, from the historical moment of the poem's composition—was coming to maturation.

6.

In a sense, Christabel finds exactly what she is looking for when she enters the forest to pray for the well-being of her betrothed—a female body and presence identified in opposition to the forces of an aristocratic patriarchy that have driven her to seek her own private means of fulfillment. And her apparent demise that results from her discovery may be read as the demise of the daughter of aristocratic patriarchy. Moreover, that the daughter who emerges to replace her—Geraldine—appears governed entirely by her own manipulative designs is a sure sign that, in the view of the poem, darker times have arisen, times that might be said to mark not only the depletion of aristocratic patriarchy but also the failure—evident even at the historical moment of their emergence—of bourgeois social structures and relations.

To cast the episodes of the poem in these terms is to raise a set of large and difficult issues having to do with romanticism's relation to feudalism, to capitalism, and to gender. While the poem seems to recognize the collapse of aristocratic patriarchy and the emergence of a new social sensibility and liberated feminine identity it laments the former and condemns the latter, and in so doing it locates itself ideologically squarely within feudal-aristocratic structures of value, seeing little hope for human accomplishment, or even integrity, outside the frames of feudal social life, including the public positioning of daughters under the law of the aristocratic father. In this vision, the poem indicates how far removed romanticism, even in the late 1790s, had become from the Enlightenment effort to construct a bourgeois public sphere and the extent to which it felt compelled to ground its vision of human possibility in precapitalist structures of authority.[25] The bourgeois ethos is rejected and even demonized (as the portrayal of Geraldine suggests) as sordid and corrupting, and the hope for human accomplishment is articulated in the imaginative and nostalgic reconstruction of the past.

While the relative merits of the backward turn of the romantic imagination are currently being debated in interesting and helpful ways, especially by scholars working in the area of German romanticism, with some scholars arguing that the romantic turn to precapitalist values is a sign of the utopian hope of romanticism and a grounds for the critique of capitalist culture,[26] I would suggest that the romantic energy of a poem such as *Christabel* is also much more than a utopian gesture that moves outside the social structures of capitalist authority. It is also a sign that the romantic imagination often was unable to look forward beyond the perceived sordidness of bourgeois reality and locate its vision in a future and better world. What in one explanation is a positive energy is in another a sign of romantic entrapment in the very ethos that it would critique and reject. The effort to see utopia in the past only, without at the same time examining the conditions that motivate a backward-looking imaginative gesture, is to risk having that utopia transmogrify into its dialectical opposite. Certainly this might be said to be the case with *Christabel,* in which the portrayal of a demonized Geraldine prevents any possibility of lifting the poem to the level of real hope: Christabel, Sir Leoline, Bracy the bard, and the castle itself all become irrevocably weakened by Geraldine's mysterious authority, to a point at which the poetic nostalgia for a beautiful and cohesive feudal world is little more than an expression of human emptiness and paralysis.

Another way to state the complexity of the romantic critique of the Enlightenment commitment to a bourgeois ethos, and to explain romanticism's nostalgic engagement with the past, is to say that even as romanticism rejects the idea of a bourgeois public sphere and subscribes to precapitalist values, as *Christabel* appears to do, at the same time it reveals the extent to which its own vision remains entrapped within the confines of its bourgeois historical moment. The desire and nostalgia that characterize the poetic voice of *Christabel,* the demonization of Geraldine, the portrayal of Christabel's innocence and beauty—these, as I have argued, are the very marks of bourgeois subjectivity, the noneconomic (cultural) expression of life within an industrial capitalist world.[27] On this view, even the romantic rejection of a bourgeois public sphere and embrace of precapitalist values are necessarily historically interwoven with the very conditions that would be transcended.

To insist on situating romantic desire squarely within the historical moment that it would overcome, however, is not to deny the political accomplishment of the romantic project or to reject the sort of progressive social critique that can be carried out from a position of romantic subjectivity. However deeply the historical energies and bourgeois assumptions of industrial capitalism are etched in the romantic imagination, its desire for a transformed world (as I have tried to show in my discussion of *Tintern Abbey* in chapter 2) is nonetheless real, and its expression of that desire carries within it potentially transformative social elements. In *Christabel,* this is seen in the fact that Geraldine, demonic though she may be in the eyes of the poem, does indeed disrupt the custom and law that entrap women and identify women entirely within the frames of masculinized feudal and aristocratic authority. Geraldine may be read as a dark bourgeois energy, but some portion of that energy is necessary in the positive transformation of the world she inhabits. Her undeniable authority, despite its negative charge, suggests the impossibility of simply overflying the conditions of the historical present and retreating into a pure and dignified past, and insofar as it does this it helps to ground the forward-looking historical possibilities of the nostalgic romantic imagination.[28]

It is perhaps appropriate to confess, by way of conclusion, that the foregoing discussion gives less attention to textual and linguistic matters than my introductory remarks had prepared for. It is certainly true that much of the argument here is grounded in rather conventional (Marxian) assumptions about the internal laws of social and historical processes and about the ideological dimensions of poetic narrative. Nevertheless, on an important level, the poststructuralist intervention shapes the argument here in significant ways. My comments about history and about the power dynamics inscribed in the narrative, for instance, begin from a refusal to valorize expressive intention; from an attempt to decenter certain humanist values that govern traditional discussions of the poem; from a recognition of the various contending narrative strategies that disrupt stable meaning; and from a recognition of certain narrative gaps and spaces that at once generate and defer meanings. Where the argument departs from certain poststructuralist claims about textuality is at the most fundamental historical level: in the last instance the argument is realist—and specifically historical materialist—in nature. In other words, the foregoing discussion assumes that poststructuralism helps to disrupt and politicize the *reading* of the narrative but that it does so, always, within the frames of real history—in this case, the history of the transition, in Britain, from an aristocratic to a bourgeois worldview.

Christabel poses the limitations, the hopes, and the historical possibilities of romantic narrative and romantic imagination, helping to elucidate the depth of the romantic desire for a world of precapitalist values, the reality of bourgeois structures of authority and belief with which that desire was obligated to contend, and the crucial—and problematic—importance of gender in the romantic effort to overmaster the severe historical pressures that both threatened and energized romantic desire. While the poem chooses to condemn the manipulative and deceitful strategies of Geraldine, it cannot but admire the uncanny effectiveness of those strategies in disrupting and collapsing the customs and laws of an older world that the poem seems to prefer; and it cannot but confess the degeneration of aristocratic patriarchy and the emergence, in the form of Geraldine, of a new and powerful feminine identity. It may be that Coleridge abandoned the poem because he saw no way to preserve the values (including those having to do with gender) of the precapitalist world that the poem would seem to cherish.[29] Nevertheless, the partial narrative that he produced—with its gaps, absences, desires, and competing meanings—tells emphatically of the ineluctable but deeply complex and troubled march of history that can be lamented or condemned but never denied; and in so doing it persuasively records the historical significance of the romantic imagination.

When placed alongside *Christabel, The Nightingale,* written at roughly the same time as Coleridge's more famous poem, appears as something more than a simple conversation poem celebrating the redemptive powers of nature.[30] Coleridge himself seemed to realize that the poem carried within it a range of possible meanings, and he was clearly concerned about how the poem might be read. When he mailed it to Wordsworth for that poet's opinion, for instance, he included a piece of doggerel verse that seems calculated in its humor to deflect attention away from the poem's complexity. But even these light rhymes display a certain anxiety about how the *Nightingale* handles a traditional set of poetic images and themes and thus, far from minimizing the seriousness of the poem, in fact call attention to it. The doggerel poem runs as follows:

> In stale blank verse a subject stale
> I send *per post* my *Nightingale;*
> And like an honest bard, dear Wordsworth,
> You'll tell me what you think, my Bird's worth.
> My opinion's briefly this—
> His *bill* he opens not amiss;
> And when he has sung a stave or so,
> His breast, & some small space below,
> So throbs & swells, that you might swear
> No vulgar music's working there.
> So far, so good; but then, 'od rot him!
> There's something falls off at his bottom.
> Yet, sure, no wonder it should breed,
> That my Bird's Tail's a tail indeed
> And makes its own inglorious harmony
> Aeolio crepitu, non carmine.

Without analyzing the particulars of these lines, it might be observed generally that they represent a psychological and rhetorical gesture not unlike the marginal gloss to the *Rime of the Ancient Mariner,* the preface to *Kubla Khan,* or the conclusion to part 2 of *Christabel,* where Coleridge anxiously tries to direct attention away from certain levels of meaning in his poetry or to place controls on how it might be read. Certainly, as a commentary on the *Nightingale,* this bit of doggerel, while expressing reasonable satisfaction with the poem, at the same time seeks to block critical access to it by backing away from, and even cursing, the overall production.

One way of getting past Coleridge's own anxiously light-hearted—almost dismissive—response to the poem and beginning to understand something of the "inglorious harmony" of its expression is by considering it as a sort of historical allegory that registers and expresses some of the troubles accompanying the large historical and social transformation articulated in *Christabel*. For while the poem, as most critics have noted, participates in the life of romantic nature philosophy and in a larger literary tradition that draws vital connections between nightingales, songs, and the poetic imagination, and while, at the level of expressive intention, it offers what Max Schulz calls a joyful affirmation of "the totality of life,"[31] it does not do so peacefully or even confidently. In fact, the relation of the poem to its literary and intellectual traditions is, on an important level, uncomfortable and even subversive, and its subversiveness is called into play quite powerfully by certain historical and social pressures that Coleridge and romanticism were compelled to negotiate. Those historical and social pressures have to do with, among other things, the relations among literary tradition, poetic voice, social class, gender, and domesticity.

The poem's troubles are perhaps most clearly pronounced in Coleridge's choice of subject matter—the nightingale—for in this choice he both acknowledges a rich literary tradition and displays the impossibility of simply drawing upon and expanding that tradition. At the level of plot, the poet describes the conventional association of the nightingale with melancholy and explains that this convention has been created, preserved, and extended by poetry:

> But some night-wandering man whose heart was pierced
> With the remembrance of a grievous wrong,
> Or slow distemper, or neglected love,
> . . . .
> . . . he, and such as he,
> First named these notes [of the nightingale] a melancholy strain.
> And many a poet echoes the conceit;
> Poet who hath been building up the rhyme
> When he had better far have stretched his limbs
> Beside a brook in mossy forest-dell. (16–26)

He then rejects this conventional poetic representation of the nightingale as a symbol of melancholy, claiming that he intends to celebrate, instead, "the merry Nightingale" (43), whose joyous voice can be plainly heard if only readers are not led astray by the conventional associations that distort the true meaning of the bird's voice. His presentation of the nightingale, then, self-consciously intervenes in literary tradition to rescue a symbol that (apparently) has long been misunderstood and misrepresented, and his celebration of the nightingale becomes a means of praising the redemptive and glorious powers of nature. The nightingale's song, as the poet describes it, is so powerful that it even draws the happy attention of children, eases the doubts and sufferings of adults, and offers some basis for hoping that joy has a place in human life.

While the surface structure of the poem offers a vision that must be acknowledged as hopeful and benevolent, at the same time the status of that vision is problematic, particularly in its relation to the deeper structures of thought that undergird it. The nature of that thought can be elucidated by considering more precisely what the poet actually does with the nightingale symbol that he appropriates for his happy vision. The melancholy nightingale that he describes in the first verse paragraph (12–39) is the nightingale associated with the myth of Philomela: "[T]hey [youths and maidens] still / Full of meek sympathy must heave their sighs / O'er Philomela's pity-pleading strains" (37–39). While the myth has taken various forms as it has passed from the Greek to Roman to English traditions, its most basic and consistently represented element involves sexual violence against women. Having been raped by Tereus, her tongue cut out to prevent her telling her story, and then on the brink of being stabbed to death by Tereus, Philomela is miraculously transformed into a nightingale, while her sister, Procne, is transformed into a swallow. The melancholy behind the nightingale's song, as Coleridge knows and acknowledges in his poem, is inextricably bound to this story of sexual violence and thus expresses a specifically feminine experience.

When Coleridge's poem invokes this traditional representation of the nightingale, only to erase it and replace it with a happier nightingale voice, he is thus calling into play a quite real gender dynamic. And the implications of Coleridge's poetic maneuvering become explicit when he engenders "the merry Nightingale" that he puts forward to replace "Philomela's pity-pleading strains":

> . . . 'Tis the merry Nightingale
> That crowds, and hurries, and precipitates
> With fast thick warbles his delicious notes,
> As he were fearful that an April night
> Would be too short for him to utter forth
> His love-chant, and disburthen his full soul
> Of all its music! (43–49)

Coleridge's intervention in literary tradition and symbolism not only entails their transformation from melancholy despair to joyous hope; it also involves their masculinization. More than this, the masculinizing energies of the poem do not transcend the sexual dynamic contained in the original nightingale myth but in fact reduplicate—at least at the level of logic and ideology—the violence that defines the original myth. These sexual matters can be glimpsed in the fact that the language used by Coleridge to describe the nightingale's "love-chant" is also used elsewhere in his poetry to suggest sexual energy. In *Kubla Khan,* for instance, the description of the life-generating energies located in "that deep romantic chasm" (12), outside the reach of the pleasure dome, is explicitly sexual:

> And from this chasm, with ceaseless turmoil seething,
> As if this earth in fast thick pants were breathing,
> A mighty fountain momently was forced. (17–19)

The statement in the *Nightingale* that the bird "precipitates / With fast thick warbles his delicious notes" of course echoes the sexual description in *Kubla Khan,* but it also reaches beyond mere sexual energy into the territory of sexual violence because the poetic context within which the statement appears recalls the original nightingale myth only to reverse the gender of the nightingale. This reversal effectively erases the gender-specific violence recorded in the original myth and installs in its place an ideological vision of a happy, love-filled masculine nightingale, whose voice silences the original story much as Tereus had tried to silence Philomela. On such a reading, it becomes clear that the pleasures described in the poem are not only sexually charged but, more specifically, derive from a sexualized poetic authority over both the melancholy voice of Philomela and the entire tradition with which she is associated.

To speak in this way may appear to be saying that the *Nightingale* is a celebratory poem about rape and that the joyful affirmation of nature's power presented on the poem's surface is simply a front for darker and more sinister concerns played out at a deeper level. While such a characterization is no doubt partly accurate, it is not the main point that I wish to make; my real concern is not to focus on the individual act of rape but rather to say that the kind of vision that the poem constructs and articulates is inherently masculinist, and that masculinist vision, in the romantic age, tends to represent its power—implicitly or explic-itly—in sexual terms. The issue, that is, is not rape as a sexual activity but rather, in Coleridge's poem, the gendered nature of power, within which not only rape but all relations of gender must be understood.

Coleridge's vision is not about gendered power in the abstract; it is about gendered power that is manipulated in specific social and historical contexts. To put the point directly, the reconstruction of myth and literary tradition that the *Nightingale* describes is at the same time the forceful poetic assertion of an individualist (masculinist) ideology. The poetic voice that governs the poem is of course the voice of romantic individualism, and it discovers its autonomy and authority everywhere it turns, whether to myth, literary tradition, or nature itself, which, in the beginning, is converted into a sort of blank canvas to be filled with the poet's new imaginings, much as literary tradition is rewritten along the lines of the poet's personal desire: "No cloud, no relique of the sunken day / Distinguishes the West, no long thin slip / Of sullen light, no obscure trembling hues" (1–3). Like Keats's portrayal of Psyche as a sort of blank canvas on which the poet imposes his shaping thoughts (see chapter 4), here nature is emphatically characterized by absence and is shown to achieve its particular meaning only by what the poet chooses to invest in it—and, as his reconstruction of the nightingale myth suggests, he chooses to invest it with his own version of its natural beauty and power.

A more particular glimpse of the historicity of poetic voice in the poem may be achieved by considering the way Coleridge develops the nightingale symbol. After establishing the masculine character of the nightingale that he wishes to celebrate, the poet immediately offers a description of a grove filled with more nightingales than are imaginable in one spot:

> . . . I know a grove
> Of large extent, hard by a castle huge,
> Which the great lord inhabits not; and so
> This grove is wild with tangling underwood
> And the trim walks are broken up, and grass,
> Thin grass and king-cups grow within the paths.
> But never elsewhere in one place I knew
> So many nightingales; and far and near,
> In wood and thicket, over the wide grove,
> They answer and provoke each other's song,
> With skirmish and capricious passagings,
> And murmurs musical and swift jug jug,

And one low piping sound more sweet than all—
Stirring the air with such a harmony,
That should you close your eyes, you might almost
Forget it was not day! (49–64)

Anxiety, desire, nostalgia, triumphant hope, and unsettling ambiguity cluster together here to provide a compelling insight into the deep historical trouble that engulfs the poem's voice and vision. For in mentioning the uninhabited castle, Coleridge (like Wordsworth, in book 1 of the *Prelude*) calls into play the very large history not simply of absentee landlords but also (as in *Christabel*) of the demise of a feudal and aristocratic social world. In the image of the vacant castle, Coleridge pinpoints this demise, and he connects it directly to the emergence of a new cultural voice—the masculine lyrical voice associated with the nightingale.

The huge number of voices in one spot, moreover, which may be said to help sing down the feudalism associated with the castle even as they nostalgically call attention to its lost grandeur, is not so much a sign of romantic collectivity as of the cultural prevalence of lyrical individualism. The focus of the poem is on the single (masculine) voice of the nightingale, and yet in the presence of the social symbolism—the castle— that might be associated with the older (feminine) nightingale myth, an entire force of voices is brought forward to illustrate the poem's point about masculine lyrical joyousness. And, as if to put the point about masculine authority beyond all doubt, the poem concludes its description of these newly triumphant voices with a brief statement about the subordinate position of nature's feminine life in relation to its masculine counterpart:

. . . On moonlight bushes,
Whose dewy leaflets are but half-disclosed,
You may perchance behold them on the twigs,
Their bright, bright eyes, their eyes both bright and full,
Glistening, while many a glow-worm in the shade
Lights up her love-torch. (64–69)

The poem, however, does not offer its vision of bourgeois masculine authority only within the contexts of myth and nature. Once the traditions of myth and literature, and the philosophy of nature, are negotiated, the poem turns dramatically toward the human, bringing its ideological commitments squarely into the arena of social life. In its description of "A most gentle Maid, / Who dwelleth in her hospitable home / Hard by the castle" (69–71), the poem describes the place and role of women in a world of authoritative masculine voice and vision. While the Maid is sympathetically drawn, as one dedicated "To something more than Nature in the grove" (73), her identity is known only through her quiet and special relation to the nightingales, which sing deliriously while she "Glides through the pathways" (74) listening to and watching their activities. While she is silent, "she knows all their notes" (74), and while she is passive,

> . . . [S]he hath watched
> Many a nightingale perch giddily
> On blossomy twig still swinging from the breeze,
> And to that motion tune his wanton song
> Like tipsy Joy that reels with tossing head. (82–86)

Like Dorothy in *Tintern Abbey*, her role seems to be the stereotypically feminine one under patriarchy: she watches and learns, silently, what masculine voices teach, and she serves, passively, as witness to the gender-specific acrobatics enlivening the world around her. Her home, meanwhile, is "hospitable" insofar as it constitutes a stable location that is receptive and responsive to the value-bestowing activities that surround it.

The poem concludes with a serene and admirable picture of domesticity that suggests, in conventional Coleridgean language, the redemptive authority of nature: even the restless and anxious child can be calmed by the soothing beauties of the natural world. But the scene is also curiously disturbing insofar as it follows immediately upon the description of the "gentle Maid, / Who dwelleth in her hospitable home" and fails to include any reference whatsoever to a mother in its portrayal of domesticity. It is as if the "gentle Maid" dwells apart even from meaningful domestic life, entirely alone and passive among the currents of masculine life that define natural and human life. When the "dear babe" (91) of the final verse paragraph experiences pain or sadness, it is the masculine poet who takes him in his arms out among the beauties of nature and the nightingale's song; indeed, the scene and the poem conclude by clustering masculine images together (the poet, the nightingales, the babe) in a way that would seem to overwhelm the earlier reference to the "gentle Maid," much as the voices of the nightingales before had overwhelmed her, breaking into song "As if some sudden gale had swept at once / A hundred airy harps" (81–82). On this view, the tale of the nightingales, no less than the tale of the babe, is emphatically "a father's tale" (106)—a tale, that is, of subjective masculine authority over the imagination, the social world, feminine identity, domestic life, and nature itself.

At the same time, while a masculine voice controls the poem from first to last, it is not monolithic, and in fact Coleridge's portrayal of an imperialistic masculine identity, extending its authority into various corners of human and natural life, carries within it a certain, potentially debilitating, anxiety. In the poem, there are three important allusions to a feminine other: Philomela, "our Sister" (40), and the "most gentle Maid." These allusions suggest, among other things, the importance of the feminine in constructing the particular masculine vision of the poem: the feminine, the poem suggests, is invoked as a sign of that which can be overcome, or transformed, by masculine imagination. It serves as a necessary source for that imagination and thus carries a certain elided authority itself.

The curious threat posed by this feminine other, even when it is apparently thoroughly subjugated, becomes clear when the fate of each feminine presence (or allusion) is considered. Philomela is invoked and then silenced, her voice giving way to a newly masculinized version of the nightingale's song; and the "gentle Maid" is presented moving out of "her hospitable home," a move that seems to clear a domestic space (seen in the subsequent lines) for masculine control. These descriptions can easily be read as acts of erasure (akin to the erasure of the original nightingale myth) in which the feminine is written into the text of the poem only to be excluded, ideologically, from the meaning and authority toward which the poem moves.

But the description of "our Sister"—Dorothy Wordsworth—departs significantly from these. Dorothy Wordsworth appears, initially, as a sort of appendage to her brother, as he alone is designated by the title "My Friend" (40); but by the end of the poem she becomes something of an equal to him in the poet's address, as they are now referred to collectively as "my friends" (110). While it is perhaps unwise to make too much of this slight change, it should not be ignored, either, for it seems to suggest the necessary (and potentially troublesome) continuing presence of the feminine in the expanding and authoritative masculine imagination. That is, what is poetically and ideologically important here is not Dorothy Wordsworth's friendship but rather the fact that her status has quietly, almost invisibly, crept upward in a manner entirely inconsistent with the larger masculine vision of the poem. As the poet invokes the feminine in order to subjugate it, he in fact constructs his dependence upon it, to the point at which it comes to occupy a silent, permanent, and potentially disruptive place *within* his imagination. He is unable to contain and control every reference that he finds necessary to his vision, as the silent modulation of Dorothy Wordsworth's status suggests. Thus, just as the poem expresses the triumph of the masculine imagination, at the same time it reveals the emergent (though difficult to see) identity of the feminine, which— appearances to the contrary—has never been entirely, or securely, situated within masculine frames of reference.

The *Nightingale* is a remarkable example of the predicament of the romantic imagination and of the gender-specific features of that predicament. As a cultural sign of the triumph of subjectivity, and—in its turn to nature—as a rejection of the capitalist transformation of society in favor of precapitalist values, romanticism was empowered by, and helped to perpetuate, bourgeois ideology, while at the same time it sought (unsuccessfully) to distance itself from the more depraved and degrading components of bourgeois society. Its expressions of hope and benevolence, therefore, as seen in a poem like the *Nightingale,* became ideologically burdened, often finding their energy and authority in the very conditions that romanticism sought to transcend or transform. Thus, in the *Nightingale,* the rejection of society in favor of nature is also a sign of the triumph of bourgeois social values; and those social values, the poem makes clear, are not only individualist but also masculinist, finding their clearest expression in an exercise of poetic power over feminine images, allusions, and, ultimately, identity. That the poem finally fails to construct a monolithic masculine vision is not a sign of Coleridge's limitations but rather a sign of the historical contradictions that define bourgeois ideology.

I want to offer a final set of comments on *The Eolian Harp* and *The Rime of the Ancient Mariner,* poems whose representations of gender are particularly troubling and enlightening. The point of drawing these poems into discussion is not to offer detailed analyses but rather to suggest certain nuances in their handling of gender that may help to bring the historical and social dimensions of Coleridge's imagination into sharper focus. For these poems, which on their surface have little to say about history and society, at the level of their deep structure put forward some of the most pressing issues facing the romantic imagination in its historical definition, and they do so in gender-specific ways.

It is a commonplace that the *Eolian Harp* constitutes an early philosophical statement that may be said to offer a premonition of Coleridge's eventual difference with Wordsworth. That statement involves Coleridge's manipulation and transformation of the lute symbol in the poem in such a way as to bespeak his intimation of the unique life-giving and value-giving powers of intellect, which, contrary to Wordsworth's later insistence, may occupy a position independent of the shaping authority of nature. It may be, in fact, according to Coleridge's poem, that nature is not a shaping authority at all but rather a secondary presence constituted wholly within the frame of "one intellectual breeze" (47), which sweeps over it and brings it into the domain of thought, and thus life. It may be, in other words, that the life, motion, and meaning of nature are products of mind. As Paul Magnuson helpfully puts it, Coleridge's vision in the *Eolian Harp* differs from Wordsworth's in that Coleridge "provides a metaphysical, rather than a material and social, ground for consciousness."[32] While Wordsworth, in his notion of a "correspondent breeze" (*Prelude* 1.35), recognizes the social and generative status of the external world, Coleridge appears to suggest that that world, or at least its value and meaning, necessarily depends upon the mind's ability to produce, enliven, and frame it.[33]

While critics are correct to investigate the poem's expressed interest in the relations between mind and nature, it is important to consider as well that it is not only a philosophical poem; its specifically intellectual interests are cast within a social framework that may alter, quite considerably, the meaning of the philosophy that occupies the surface structure of the poem. I am of course speaking here of the domestic context within which Coleridge situates his speculative comments and which ultimately overwhelms intellectual speculation entirely, calling the poet's attention emphatically back to more traditional and orthodox ways of thinking about the relations between the mind and nature: intellect is given over, finally, in favor of "Faith that inly *feels*" (60), and that faith is associated with Sara, who "healed me, / . . . / . . . and gave me to possess / Peace, and this Cot, and thee, heart-honour'd Maid!" (61–64).

The poem's comments on Sara have most often been used as a ground from which to offer a negative commentary on her narrow-minded and constraining effort to control the intellectual accomplishment toward which Coleridge appears to be moving in the poem. In fact, however, Sara functions precisely in the manner prescribed to her by the poet, and this fact carries significant interpretative weight.[34] She is a constraining presence only insofar as she is portrayed as such; she is not an agent in the poem but rather a character who is made to function within the larger structure of the poem's vision—that is, she functions in a particular relation to the other textual and ideological components of the poem. It is therefore inappropriate to view her as an intrusion, an obstacle, or a constraining presence who undermines the poem's real philosophical concerns when in fact she is poetically constructed in such a way as to point the direction of at least one thread of the poem's meaning. On this view, the philosophy of mind with which the poet appears to be preoccupied must be placed within, and alongside, the domestic picture of the poet and Sara; it must be understood as an interest whose meanings arise and take shape within the context of domesticity that the poem itself puts forward.

One way of getting at the various expressions, tensions, and ideas in the poem that are suggested by Sara's characterization is by considering that the poem's various details of intellectual and domestic life carry within them a set of larger concerns having to do (to state the matter bluntly) with the relations between an imperialistic imagination, sexual desire, and gender hierarchy. That is, the speculative philosophy that stands at the center of the poem registers the poet's own sense of tremendous intellectual power to penetrate the deepest questions of meaning in the universe or actually to construct meaning; the "intellectual breeze" that his own mind appears to have discovered may sweep over the entire universe as a "God," generating the thoughts of, and assigning values to, "all of animated nature" (44). Such a vision is predicated upon the assumption that the mind's home is not local but universal, that the mind is not responsible simply for itself, as its authority sweeps over the vast world, mastering all that it encounters. The poet's mind, in other words, appears to constitute a sort of imperialistic, ever expanding authority that is free to embark on imaginative journeys of discovery and then to assign a particular meaning to that which happens to be discovered.

Further, the possibilities associated with speculative philosophy in the poem are described, in one place, in graphically sexual terms, suggesting that an intense desire stands behind the poet's imagining mind, not unlike the desire portrayed in the *Nightingale*:

> And that simplest Lute,
> Placed length-ways in the clasping casement, hark!
> How by the desultory breeze caress'd,
> Like some coy maid half yielding to her lover,

It pours such sweet upbraiding, as must needs
Tempt to repeat the wrong! And now, its strings
Boldlier swept, the long sequacious notes
Over delicious surges sink and rise. (12–19)

What is remarkable about this passage is not that it describes a masculine vision of sexuality—a point that could perhaps be argued either way—but rather that it describes libidinal energy at all as a starting point for philosophical speculation. According to the motivating assumptions of this passage, the intellectual project with which the poem is engaged both desires and requires libidinal energy to enliven the mind and to energize its expansive possibilities. The imagining mind looks first to libidinal life for its inspiration and then puts that life in the service of intellectual speculation. According to this poetic formulation, libido is a sign of the triumph and authority of the imagination, which displays its ability both to control and use an energy source that is necessary to the sort of intense philosophical life that the poem attempts to describe.

At the same time, however, the act of calling sexuality into play apparently calls into play as well a possible threat to the intellectual mastery imagined by the poet. Even in the moment of eroticizing the lute image, the poet displays a certain anxiety insofar as he views sexual pleasure, in this context, as "wrong" (17). The guilt, or anxiety, here is extremely problematic to the poem's vision, for in backing away, however slightly, from the free flow of libidinal energy that the poet himself has called into play, he is offering a moral judgment against that which, according to his own profession, makes possible "joyance every where" (29). Whatever one may wish to say about the passage as autobiography—that is, about Coleridge's personal sexual confusion—the ideological point here is that sexual guilt and desire, aggression and fear, confidence and anxiety mark the poetic effort to produce the sort of large philosophical vision to which (the poet seems to feel) his mind has a legitimate claim; and this uncertainty results, at least in part, from the fact that he is not confident that he can control, absolutely, the vast sexual territory that he has begun to open up. Sexual energy is both desirable and necessary to the poet's expanding vision, but it also constitutes a bold and potentially uncontrollable life that feels wrong for the vision that it enables.

In light of this understanding of the poem's speculative section, the portrayal of the highly domestic and orthodox Sara becomes clear. In backing away from intellectual speculation, the poet is not simply backing away from blasphemous philosophy, nor is he succumbing, against his better sense, to a narrow-minded and petty spouse. Rather, he is retreating from a frightful and sexualized territory of potentially disruptive energies and possibilities into a happily desexualized and safe domestic territory, with its clearly prescribed boundaries of orthodox belief, love, and value. That Sara can be read as petty and pouting serves poetic retreat well, for her characterization effectively covers over the poet's own guilt over the world he has begun to mark out for himself. In backing away from the large vision that he had begun to construct, and from the libidinal energy that had enlivened that vision, he is not showing himself as a faithful husband to a small-minded wife; he is, rather, busily constructing a smaller world over which he may have firmer control. The god of this smaller world, the poet himself says,

> . . . with his saving mercies healed me,
> A sinful and most miserable man,
> Wilder'd and dark, and gave me to possess
> Peace, and this Cot, and thee, heart-honour'd Maid! (61–64)

This description is marked, clearly, by the idea of possession, and the very Sara who appears to control his wandering mind is one of the poet's possessions. In her are represented values and beliefs that provide a sure and safe anchor for the poet's adventurous desire and speculation; her meekness and her simple faith offer a necessary retreat from the risks involved in following "vain Philosophy's aye-babbling spring" (57). She constitutes a domestic space that the poet may occupy and possess. She is, in short, not an autonomous subject calling her free-thinking husband back from the dangerous and blasphemous grasp of philosophical speculation but rather a carefully drawn subordinate character constructed entirely by the poet to serve particular ideological needs. He makes her into an object that both provides him with emotional security and effectively draws attention away from his own manipulative authority.

To view the poem in this way is not to deny the importance of the particular sort of speculative philosophy with which it is engaged but rather to suggest that matters of intellect are often vividly caught up in matters of ideology, which are always social. The speculative mind, as Coleridge presents it, operates in imperialist fashion, moving into and across new territories that have yet to be charted and valued, only to discover that imperialism often calls into play threatening and disruptive energies (and for Coleridge those energies are often sexual).[35] Anxious retreat, however, does not signify abandonment of imperialistic drive but rather, in the *Eolian Harp*, a momentary resetting of poetic sights on a lower and surer territory, which can be controlled and valued to meet the particular needs of poetic identity.

If in matters of style and content they are radically dissimilar, in their ideological structure the *Rime of the Ancient Mariner* and the *Eolian Harp* are remarkably alike, suggesting something of the extent to which Coleridge's imagination, at least in the 1790s, was gripped by questions of gender and power. While the Mariner's killing of the albatross may be the central plot-level event in the poem, the main event for the poem's meaning, as critics since Bostetter have recognized,[36] is the description of the skeleton ship carrying Death and Life-in-Death. The darkness and terror associated with this episode are an explicit and disturbing extreme example of what the imperialist imagination may discover beyond the secure borders of domestic life and faith, and the poet responds to that discovery in the same way that he responds to the much less threatening intellectual possibilities portrayed in the *Eolian Harp*—that is, by retreating rapidly into the secure arms of domesticity and conventional religious belief. At the end of the poem, the Mariner celebrates his return to "mine own countree" (467) and lectures the stunned Wedding-Guest on the virtues of living and worshipping in a religion-based community. From the Mariner's point of view, at least, the adventure of discovery into the unknown produces more complications and threats than he is capable of mastering, and thus they are best avoided by looking closer to home for personal happiness and reward.[37]

But here, as in the *Eolian Harp*, Coleridge does not appear to reject the imperialist imagination; rather he acknowledges its tremendous powers and then seeks to contain those powers within a scheme of benevolence, compassion, and traditional values. However, containment is at best only partially successful, as at the end of the poem the Mariner's satisfaction is offset powerfully by the Wedding-Guest's deep sadness. The very elements that have been called into play by the Mariner's narrative to demonstrate the integrity of domesticity and conservative religion haunt the poem to its very conclusion, creating the impression that once desire ventures beyond the safe borders of community, its discoveries can never be returned to their undiscovered state; even while discovery may feed one's personal commitment to the virtues of domesticity, at the same time, by its very otherness, it threatens those virtues.[38]

The particular representation of this commonly understood set of problems bears on the issue of gender in several important ways. In some respects, in fact, the crisis of the imagination portrayed in the poem is the crisis of sexual power within the frame of social transformation. The poem is an extremely masculine story of discovery, despair, and triumph: the Mariner; the two hundred crew mates; the Pilot, Pilot's boy, and Hermit; the Wedding-Guest—the representation of human meaning always bears most pressingly upon men. And yet the Mariner's central and most profound encounter in the narrative is with a strange and powerful female presence, and this encounter determines absolutely all subsequent interpretative matters.

It is worth noting that the narrative itself calls particular attention to the gender issue insofar as prior to the arrival of the skeleton ship virtually all associations in the poem are masculine. The Mariner and the Wedding-Guest, of course, constitute a human masculine presence early on. But the various depictions of nature, too, are drawn in distinctly masculine terms, a fact that seems at odds, for instance, with Wordsworth's typical characterizations of nature:

> "And now the STORM-BLAST came, and he
> Was tyrannous and strong." (41–42)
> . . . .
> The Sun now rose upon the right:
> Out of the sea came he. (83–84)
> . . . .
> And some in dreams assure were
> Of the Spirit that plagued us so;
> Nine fathom deep he had followed us
> From the land of mist and snow. (131–34)

Prior to the arrival of the skeleton ship, the bride is the only feminine being to which the poem alludes (33–36), and she is securely positioned within a pervasive and defining masculine authority.

With the arrival of the skeleton ship, however, masculine authority suddenly dissipates as feminine images and references are clustered together in a manner that seems to produce an overpowering, monolithic, and horrific new authority:

> Alas! (thought I, and my heart beat loud)
> How fast she nears and nears!
> Are those *her* sails that glance in the Sun,
> Like restless gossameres?

Are those *her* ribs through which the Sun
Did peer, as through a grate?
And is that Woman all her crew?
Is that a DEATH? and are there two?
Is DEATH that woman's mate?
Her lips were red, *her* looks were free,
Her locks were yellow as gold:
Her skin was as white as leprosy,
The Night-mare LIFE-IN-DEATH was she,
Who thicks Man's blood with cold. (181–94)

Perhaps the most stunning passage in all of Coleridge's poetry, these lines capture the shocked poetic recognition of unavoidable feminine presence, even feminine libidinal presence. The shock is so overpowering that, after Life-in-Death wins the Mariner in the dice game, even the most masculine component of nature itself, the sun, seems to be defeated—"The Sun's rim dips; the stars rush out: / At one stride comes the dark" (199–200)—and a maddened feminized nature in the form of the moon seems to take over:

Till clomb above the eastern bar
The horned Moon, with one bright star
Within the nether tip.
One after one, by the star-dogged Moon,
Too quick for groan or sigh,
Each turned his face with a ghastly pang,
And cursed me with his eye. (208–15)

The dread with which the Mariner is overcome is, on some level, a sexual dread because Life-in-Death is a curiously sexual character. Her red lips, her yellow hair, her deathly white skin, and her free looks all bespeak libidinal energy and feminine authority, which is to say that, for the Mariner, they are signs of the death of masculine power and thus produce masculine horror and dread.

It is this demonic feminine, which the Mariner has, in effect, sought out and discovered, that the poem seeks to contain. The remainder of the poem, therefore, diminishes and disperses the feminine libidinal energy that has been discovered to lurk in the outer reaches of the masculine imperialist imagination, at once desired and loathed, at once both a saving and a potentially destructive reality. As the Mariner's own ship is transformed into a feminized skeleton ship, inhabited by masculine Life-in-Death and Death, it comes under the firm control of the masculine Spirit beneath the sea and the restored masculine sun above: "The Sun, right up above the mast, / Had fixed her to the ocean" (383–84). The moon's madness, too, passes, and is put in the service of the Mariner: "[S]he guides him smooth or grim, / See, brother, see! how graciously / She looketh down on him" (419–21). And upon his return home the Mariner applauds what he perceives to be the proper hierarchal relations of gender within a stable patriarchal social order:

> O sweeter than the marriage-feast,
> 'Tis sweeter far to me,
> To walk together to the kirk
> With a goodly company!—
> To walk together to the kirk,
> And all together pray,
> While each to his great Father bends,
> Old men, and babes, and loving friends
> And youths and maidens gay! (601–9)

Like the *Nightingale,* the *Rime* is finally a "father's tale," a poem about the need to contain feminine life and energy, even as feminine otherness is essential to masculine identity. But what Coleridge's poetry appears to know about this peculiar patriarchal arrangement, within a larger frame of imperialist expansion (both of the mind and of the state), is that it is always subject to the threat of the very feminine energy upon which it depends for its existence. This is why so many of Coleridge's poems that offer happy endings, with the (masculine) world carefully preserved, in fact read like prescriptions for absolute imprisonment.

Chapter Four

Keats

Recent critical investigation of the relations between Keats and history has raised several difficult kinds of questions that Keats scholars have yet to address fully.[1] What do we mean, for instance, when we speak of Keats and history? Do we mean only the history of political events in Keats's age and the representation of these events in his poems?[2] Or do we mean literary history: the relation of Keats's poetry to, and its place within, the tradition of classical and English literature?[3] Or does the word *history* push us into areas of extraliterary concern to include social history, the place of Keats's poetry within the frames of everyday economic and ideological life?[4] Is Keats's poetry itself not only a literary object but also a social-historical object?

More problematically, can the term *history* be said to designate only matters from the past? Must it not also designate something in addition, namely the historical position from which current criticism attempts to understand Keats? Does historical criticism of Keats, in other words, include among its self-conscious assumptions that difficult activity of appropriating poetic texts from the past, so that what is historical about Keats's poetry is, in part, its interpretation? If critical activity itself must be understood historically, then to what extent are the scholar and critic of Keats implicated in the historical situation that surrounds the pro-duction *and reception* of Keats's poetry?

Also troubling for historical investigation is the meaning of the word *Keats*. When we speak of Keats, do we mean a lower-middle-class Englishman, roughly five feet tall, who was a friend of Charles Cowden Clarke, trained at Guy's Hospital as an apothecary, wrote a small body of beautiful poems, and died of tuberculosis at the age of twenty-five?

Or do we mean, more abstractly, a cultural idea whose authority automatically assigns certain meanings and values to poetic texts when the name Keats is set in relation to those texts? Moreover, are the historical meanings of Keats's poetry determined absolutely by the name Keats? To what extent does Keats—as person or cultural idea—control the critical investigation of poems traditionally associated with his name, and to what extent ought (can) that investigation resist the constraints that the name of Keats might impose?

In what follows, I want to examine the *Ode to Psyche* in an attempt to specify some of the larger issues associated with such questions about Keats and history, particularly issues having to do with ideology, social relations, and sexual power. While I acknowledge the contributions made by the rich tradition of Keats scholarship, the relevance of Keats's expressed intentions with respect to one level of the poem's meaning, and the integrity of the vision thematized in the poem,[5] my investigation begins elsewhere, namely with the materialist assumption that criticism necessarily finds its richest territory of meaning at the level of a poem's deep structure. At this level one finds not only major sources of poetic inspiration but also certain socially charged currents of meaning that often contradict—even while they shape—poetic expression; for at this level of the poetic text, the dialectics of history are registered and play themselves out prior to their reconciliation and resolution at the level of theme and imagination.

1.

The primary deep historical pressure operating on *Psyche*—and, more generally, as I have argued throughout the present study, on British romanticism—involves the demise of aristocratic feudalism and the triumph of industrial capitalism and bourgeois ideology in the late eighteenth and early nineteenth centuries.[6] One motivating desire in Keats's poetry, including *Psyche,* is to shape meaning out of, and express hope in the face of, certain powerful political, economic, and cultural conditions associated with this historical transformation: the quantifying pressures of an emergent and powerful commercialism that would subsume all things of quality (including poetry itself) and transform them into commodities to be exchanged on the open market; an increasingly militarized state apparatus established to secure and extend the operations of capital; the demise of religion as a master discourse and its replacement by an individualist ethic grounded in cash nexus; new forms of government repression; rampant urbanization and its accompanying problems of escalating unemployment and poverty.[7] Under such historical conditions and pressures as these, a poem such as *Psyche,* which describes its titular goddess as a member of a "faded hierarchy" (25) and as a beautiful, noble victim of a declining world, is more than a poetic celebration of a goddess out of classical mythology.[8] It is more, even, than a nostalgic expression of pure love. It is also, necessarily, a symbolic representation of the deep structural realities constituent of the world in which Keats produced the poem, the decline of Psyche's world registering the decline of another world before the poet's eyes—the world of aristocratic feudalism. The descriptions of Psyche and the ambitious and noble vision of human warmth and love reach beyond the poem's classical subject matter to form a series of anxious responses to the social instability of Keats's own day, responses which range from disenchantment to hope that a new world order might provide heretofore unseen opportunities and possibilities.[9] The poem finds in the story of Psyche reasons to insist that love and integrity are humanly attainable, but at the same time it expresses an equally strong apprehension that "in these days so far retir'd / From happy pieties" (40–41) the imagination may be unable to achieve the beautiful idealisms that the poet would associate with Psyche.

Some of the anxieties that characterize the poem are suggested in the opening few lines, though their social and historical dimensions are not immediately visible. By way of beginning, the poet asks that his lines be heard by Psyche; states that the poem itself has been "wrung" (1) from him, albeit by "sweet enforcement" (2); and asks the object of the poet's admiration to "pardon" (3) him for the content of his poem. In addition to displaying personal nervousness arising from the poet's encounter with the figure of Psyche, these opening comments suggest a historical nervousness; that is, the anxiety here arises in part from the poet's sense of his own existence in a world lacking the faith and intense imagination—a world "far retir'd / From happy pieties"—that allegedly existed in the past. The extreme incongruity that the poet imagines between his own degraded world and the rich classical past is psychologically disorienting, as is evidenced in his desire to enjoy the beauties associated with that past and his focus on one particular moment that reminds him of its demise. It is as though the poet hopes that recollection and exaltation of a character such as Psyche from the classical past might revivify a modern world that he believes has lost its enchanting qualities, and yet, as early as the opening lines, he betrays his doubt that this is possible.

To read the poem's anxieties as an articulation of the incongruity between the modern and classical worlds helps to elucidate a more particular (though barely visible) determining pressure on Keats's imagination. Even as the poem struggles to overcome anxiety by describing a world of imaginative possibilities—by nobly attempting to create a world of freedom out of a world of necessity—it remains transfixed by the claims of the present, especially by the cultural authority of commodity exchange. Under that authority the poem circulates within specific social networks—economic and ideological—and its *value* is determined by its circulatory path. Its *meanings,* moreover, are conditioned, in significant ways, by the kinds of value that are attached to it by commodity culture.[10] I am not suggesting, of course, that the poem is a commodity in the crudest sense, produced for sale on the open market, but simply that its value and meanings arise from *within,* and are shaped by, frames of cultural reference governed and shaped by commodity exchange. Keats's poem competes for ideological space within these frames of reference, and in so doing it necessarily registers their values, assumptions, and logic.

Before approaching the specific significance of this argument for *Psyche,* I want to recast it in slightly different terms in an attempt to situate the poem more clearly among its determining social relations. Marx defines the commodity, generally, as "an object outside us, a thing that by its properties satisfies human wants of some sort or another. The nature of such wants, whether, for instance, they spring from the stomach or from fancy, makes no difference."[11] The commodity, moreover, possesses two forms—"a physical or natural form, and a value-form"—the latter of which is characterized by "a purely social reality."[12] That is, the value of the commodity is never inherent to itself but always depends upon its social situation. To insist upon the social embeddedness of the commodity's value is, among other things, to secularize it, to deny that there is a "universal equivalent"[13] of value in some transsocial or transhistorical sphere that is a measure of the value of all commodities. If there is to be a universal equivalent of value, according to Marx, then society itself must create it.[14]

Under capitalism, the commodity takes on an even more specific meaning than I have described above, one determined by the paths of bourgeois social relations along which it circulates. No longer an objective product meant only to satisfy some human need, the commodity comes to be defined, rather, in terms of its relation to other commodities as an exchange value. As Marx puts it, "The circulation of commodities is the starting point of capital."[15] The commodity is now bought and sold in the open market, valued not for its use but for its perceived ability to contribute to an escalating process of exchange and accumulation. Under capitalism, use value is given over in favor of exchange value, and as this occurs the products of human labor lose their human character and are transformed into ostensibly discrete units, the sole purpose of which is to find an authoritative position within the market. With the emergence of exchange value, human labor itself is thus transformed from a qualitative into a quantitative value as it becomes inextricably attached to the demands and definition of commodity exchange: human labor becomes reified, alienated, and broken into units capable of being managed by the culture and economics of exchange value.[16]

To view *Psyche* within the terms of commodity exchange is to say that it is an objective product of human labor that performs a human function, that its value is social value alone, and that its precise social value is determined by its circulatory path. Its circulatory path, moreover, as defined by exchange value, sets limits to both its formal and expressive character according to the social and cultural demands of exchange. Expressive intention, textual detail, and poetic beauty, for instance, arise from within these parameters, and to the extent that they do so they are quantities, abstracted from human practice and transformed into isolated "things" to satisfy the demands of commodity culture. This is not, again, to say that *Psyche* is a poem about buying and selling but rather that its vision must be understood within the historical and cultural reality of buying and selling—that is, within the social reality of reification and alienation.

This is admittedly a sterile and grim view of poetry that does not explain all that poetry is or might become. Poetry is also, as *Psyche* is, a real expression of human need and desire, and as such it possesses a utopian dimension that (one might hope) is potentially socially transformative. But not to situate Keats's poem among the specific social relations that enable and control its value and meaning may reduce its social function to the mystification of social relations—absorbing the contradictions of social life and resolving them into a nostalgic vision of what once was but never more shall be.

While in *Psyche* there are no overt plot-level references to the marketplace that might clearly demonstrate its position within a culture of commodity exchange, the poem nonetheless forcefully reveals at least one of the major ideological features of commodity culture. The poem's vision of transcendental possibility is ineluctably grounded in a specifically bourgeois sensibility consonant with the capitalist economic order of commodity exchange. It is a sensibility characterized most impressively (I am here relying on Jameson's description) by "that rich, monadic, properly psychological autonomy" of the individual subject.[17] That autonomy assumes, among other things, that the individual is an isolated being circulating along various social paths freely chosen by itself. (As I shall argue, however, one path that is not—and cannot—be chosen within such a system is the path of communal hope: the individual can enter society, but only as one subject among an aggregate of other subjects.) The price of this individual autonomy, ultimately, is the utter privatization of human life, insofar as the subjective vision of transcendental possibility requires the exchange of the social world for isolation and the conversion of human value into a small, discrete territory of pleasure meant for consumption only by the individual subject. In *Psyche*, this point is driven home by the poet's acceptance of a shrunken territory for imaginative play; the world, which the poet asserts has lost its enchanting quality, is given over in favor of "some untrodden region of my mind" (51), which he believes will be furnished with his self-generated emblems of value. Standing hauntingly behind this vision, in mystified form, are the sure loss of community, the isolation of the individual from the social world, and the conversion of human desire into a medium of exchange and consumption, wherein collective hope is sold in return for a private world of private pleasure.

The argument that I am presenting here about the isolation and commodification of human value in *Psyche* echoes one part of Christopher Caudwell's reading of Keats. Describing romanticism as that phase of the "bourgeois illusion" ushered in by the industrial revolution, Caudwell says that "Keats is the first great poet to feel the strain of the poet's position . . . as producer for the free market."[18] That strain "led him to a position which was to set the keynote for future bourgeois poetry: 'revolution' as a flight *from* reality. Keats is the bannerbearer of the Romantic Revival. The poet now escapes upon the 'rapid wings of poesy' to a world of romance, beauty and sensuous life separate from the poor, harsh, real world of everyday life, which it sweetens and by its own loveliness silently condemns."[19] While his description of Keats as a poet given to imaginative flight from reality is certainly too reductive, as recent criticism has begun to show,[20] Caudwell is correct to stress that Keats's poetry is mediated in important ways by the social and historical energies of an emergent industrial capitalism (particularly those energies that isolate the imagination, reducing it to a private form that can be effectively managed by the demands of commodity exchange) and that these energies are manifested in the very *aesthetic* qualities of Keats's imagination. The value, desire, and hope expressed in Keats's poetry (no less than its expressions of despair, disenchantment, and hardship) are *real* enough, but their shape and content are never independent of the historical situation (that is, industrial capitalism) within which they emerge.

Caudwell's point can be sharpened by casting it more specifically in terms of *Psyche:* the demise of Psyche's world, Keats emphasizes, has left her homeless and at the mercy of forces out of her control (28–35), just as the demise of aristocracy has left the poet spiritually homeless. Born into the modern world that Caudwell describes, the poet has lost the faith that he imagines must have belonged to an earlier age; as he describes it, he is "too late for antique vows" and "Too, too late for the fond believing lyre" (36–37). The only region remaining for his faith and hope, as for Wordsworth before him,[21] is the "untrodden region of my mind." This being the case, it is not surprising that the poem energetically (and hopefully) explores this uncharted region at the same time that it betrays an uncomfortable conviction that discovery of this new region is more than the discovery of a new source of inspiration and potential value: it is also a realization that the modern world has been lost to an unseen and unspoken—yet definitive—authority that has left *only* the mind in the control of individuals.[22]

If the poet finds a way in *Psyche* to allay his anxieties by celebrating his imaginative ability to revive and invest with new meaning a character from the mythic past, thereby providing a momentary resistance to the quantifying pressures of his own world, subsequent readers of Keats (from T. S. Eliot to Earl Wasserman to Helen Vendler) have followed much the same path. By accepting the poet's definition of what counts as meaningful and elaborating it in a vocabulary consistent with the demands of modern critical sensibility, scholars and critics have done much to preserve and disseminate the beautiful imaginings in Keats's poetry. But, as McGann has shown,[23] they have done so at great cost, for their intellectual labors often tend to exclude consideration of the determining historical conditions (as described by Caudwell, for instance) with which Keats's imagination contended. This exclusion means not only that the understanding of Keats today remains incomplete but also that the loss of the world, registered in a poem like *Psyche*, is also the loss of today's world: criticism remains as much a private enterprise as Keats's poem, tending to seek its purpose away from a world that no longer cares to hear its voice.

2.

I want now to consider, more specifically, how *Psyche* articulates some of the historical currents and pressures that I have just sketched. One obvious feature of the poem's imaginative struggle with (and within) history is its tendency to appropriate the past and convert it into nostalgia. However true it may be that Psyche and Cupid's world is forever lost—and the poem does not deny this fact—the *recollection* of that world is rich with a sense of past greatness far surpassing anything found in the present. The curious paradox of this imaginative maneuver is seen, for instance, in the fact that as soon as the poet catalogs Psyche's lack of the various riches that would be becoming to a goddess (24–35), and, generally, describes her unfortunate fate at the hands of her world, he forgets the darkness inherent in his vision of the past. More than this, he liquidates the past of its burdens by bringing them forward as a commentary on his own world, which he believes is imaginatively and spiritually dead:

> O brightest! though too late for antique vows,
> Too, too late for the fond believing lyre,
> When holy were the haunted forest boughs,
> Holy the air, the water, and the fire;
> Yet even in these days so far retir'd
> From happy pieties, thy lucent fans,
> Fluttering among the faint Olympians,
> I see, and sing, by my own eyes inspired. (36–43).

This maneuver completed, he swiftly turns his attention once again to the past, imaginatively recreating it as stable, inviting, and rich in possibility.

But of course the imaginative recreation of Psyche's world is not really so much a retreat into the past as it is a labor to make an idealized vision of the past available as a redemptive power for the present. Like all nostalgia, this poetic move attempts to create a space where loneliness is at least temporarily laid to rest and alienation is defeated. With his own world much too threatening to negotiate imaginatively, the poet remakes the long-dead world of the mythic past, which can offer but little resistance. He brings this world forward into "some untrodden region of my mind," where it serves well, if only for the life of the poem, as raw material for expressing what he would like to find, but cannot, in his own world. And he shapes that material as he would like to shape, but cannot, his world, which, he stresses, has been spiritually and imaginatively set adrift.

I am offering here perhaps an unduly strong explanation of the troubled energies moving through the poem and perhaps an unnecessarily negative representation of the shaping powers of Keats's imagination. But the point in casting my position in these terms is not to destroy the poem's clear expressions of hope and possibility. It is rather to suggest, realistically, the historical logic governing Keats's imagination and thereby to elucidate the besetting conditions under which his imaginative vision of hope was produced. Everywhere in this poem about classical fictions and the inner recesses of the individual modern mind are traces of a troubling reality characterized by the conflict between myth and history, present and past, the individual and the world—by the conflict between the *form* of Keats's imagination and certain unspoken historical currents that make that particular form possible. The poem admittedly *desires* freedom and happiness, but it can give shape to that desire only in accordance with a material situation that insistently obstructs freedom and happiness. Therefore, until that situation is known, the nature of the desire arising from it cannot be fully understood.

3.

In what I have been saying about an unspoken, though authoritative, historical presence in *Psyche,* where does Keats the poet fit? Within the frame of the foregoing discussion, does authorial intention become insignificant? The short answer to these questions is that intention remains crucially important, though not in the way that criticism of Keats perhaps once assumed. It matters that Keats *chose* Psyche as his subject matter; that he believed he was writing a poem that, in its vision, surpassed the work of writers (such as Mrs. Tighe) whom he once greatly admired; that he relied for information on the writings of Apuleius and Lemprière; that he knew he was celebrating a "hethen [sic] Goddess" (*LJK* 2:106).[24] Such details and others, long known to Keats scholars, are important not only because they provide information about Keats's intellectual interests and psychological quirks but more importantly because they help to focus one level of historical interest in the poem. That Keats was drawn to things Hellenic and pagan as possible subjects for expressing his understanding of beauty and truth says a great deal about the shape of the romantic world, both what some romantic writers considered its paucity of attractive current topics for poetry and its standing challenge to poets to shape vision out of conditions "too late for the fond believing lyre" (37).[25] Keats's intentions and motives are important, in short, because they are one set of details that might inform us about the *genesis* of the poem.[26]

Authorial intention, however, is ultimately contingent rather than constitutive, though this fact does not make it any less important or illuminating in historical terms. It is one condition of meaning within a larger set of historical conditions of meaning, and its precise significance for literary study is that it focuses and enlivens—even as it may threaten to mystify—the historical situation out of which it is born. In the case of *Psyche*, Keats's intentions, recorded in his letter to George and Georgiana Keats (*LJK* 2:105–9), help readers to understand the sorts of choices available to him as a poet in post-Waterloo England.

The issue of intention, or at least of authorial presence, may be elucidated by reference to Keats's famous "vale of soul-making" letter, which immediately precedes the transcription of *Psyche* for his brother and sister-in-law. This letter is one of Keats's most eloquent statements describing his impatience with orthodox Christian explanations of human life and his sense of the extent to which material circumstance shapes and empowers, in fundamental ways, human value, hope, and activity. As such, it provides a helpful gloss on certain ideas uppermost in his mind at the time he composed *Psyche*.

At the center of the "vale of soul-making" letter are two major concerns that suggest the intellectual position at which Keats, following Hazlitt, had begun to arrive in 1819: *identity* and *circumstance*. In his three-part formulation—intelligence, human heart, world—meant to describe the major features and processes of human experience, Keats not only asserts the determining role that material circumstance plays in human life ("man was formed by circumstances" [*LJK* 2:103]) but, more importantly, seeks to explain why the authority of circumstance is proper, necessary, and *valuable* in human life ("Do you not see how necessary a World of Pains and troubles is to school an Intelligence and make it a soul?" [*LJK* 2:102]). In laying out this argument he knowingly distances himself from a Christian explanation that would see human life as irretrievably fallen, and capable of salvation only by professions of faith and prayers calling for the aid of a transhistorical redemptive power. Unlike Christianity, he says, the "system of Salvation" that he imagines "does not affront our reason and humanity" (*LJK* 2:102) because it acknowledges, embraces, and finds a way to exist meaningfully within circumstances that, in Keats's view, provide the necessary bases of human knowledge and capacity.

In laying out this explanation of human salvation, Keats focuses directly on the question of identity and is particularly concerned to show that identity is not pregiven but rather emerges from situations of conflict and difficulty. His account approaches what would now be called a materialist explanation of identity and goes a long way toward rewriting certain assumptions about identity that had governed the vision of some poets only a generation earlier, especially Wordsworth. But the explanation that he offers is itself implicated in the very circumstances that it is meant to address, so that its materialist intention is only partly realized. That is, the explanation, while rejecting Wordsworth's view of the defining authority of the individual imagination, points toward a view of identity as a happy gathering of troubled circumstantial pressures into an untroubled and spiritually meaningful essence: identity becomes synonymous with salvation, and thus it is, finally, but a modified version of the Christian idealism to which Keats objects.

Keats's position articulates the force of a desire to believe that turbulent circumstance can and does produce intelligence, identity, and soul, all of which, for him, constitute the center of human meaning and purpose. Such desire is, on some level, itself a response to and product of circumstance, which, on its own terms, cannot guarantee the fulfillment of which Keats speaks. In fact, his effort to cut through the forms of idealism governing much of the intellectual thought of his age actually duplicates that thought insofar as it assumes that individual identity is an essence corresponding to a transhistorical essence (God). Keats's effort advances an idea of circumstance, drawing life from its determining presence (felt anew with particular force at the moment of severe social crisis in post-Waterloo Europe) while at the same time retreating from the world of circumstance into a nostalgic notion of identity as a territory of overriding meaning, possibility, and reward.

The concept of identity that Keats advances corresponds roughly to the bourgeois concept of individual subjectivity and autonomy, disclosing yet again Keats's inability to think beyond the categories available to him within a commodified, reified, and alienating culture. The "vale of soul-making" letter describes a search for individual human meaning, and that search is obsessed with identity, which, Keats insists, stands the best shot of settling the difficult conflicts tearing at the world. The letter, in other words, is an act of individual subject construction, motivated by a conviction that "*Intelligence* [is] *destined to possess the sense of Identity* (*LJK* 2:102; Keats's emphasis). According to this logic, whatever Keats might say about the determining authority of circumstance, that authority is in fact always secondary rather than determining, and the real authority is an individual identity capable of shaping circumstance to its own ends. While it is asserted that circumstance is pivotal to Keats's argument, it is cast as that which serves the individual subject, which is Keats's real concern, and in this respect the materialist edge of his argument is dulled.

The "vale of soul-making" letter is important to *Psyche* because it helps to elucidate Keats's strong drive to situate himself as a stable identity in a disjointed world. This is precisely what he attempts in *Psyche,* which might be regarded as a poetic representation of the idea of soul described in the letter. The relation between these two documents is seen not only in the obvious attention that Keats gives, in the poem, to Psyche as soul or in his exploration of the soul's home in "some untrodden region of my mind." It is seen, more compellingly, in the laborious process of soul-making that he describes in the poem's final stanza. Here the poet describes himself as dedicated to "build[ing] a fane / In some untrodden region of my mind" (50–51); his efforts will be enabled by "a working brain" (60), whose "shadowy thought" (65) will "win" (65) what it can for the soul. Such dedication, carried out entirely within the frame of the individual mind, will, it is hoped, produce a mental territory—an intelligence and a soul—where love can dwell in luxurious warmth.

This final stanza of *Psyche* allows one to see clearly what goes largely unremarked in the letter, namely the active *construction* of identity. The poem traces, in imaginative form, the world of circumstance—with its enforcements (2), "surprise" (8), spiritual void (36–41), and "pleasant pain" (52)—and, at the same time, it describes the process of producing identity out of circumstance. Moreover, that identity is emphatically shown to be individual rather than communal, with its desires, integrity, love, and hope housed entirely within the private mind. It is as though circumstance is a necessary starting point for the poet, but only that; circumstance is eventually abandoned in favor of the mind's imaginings that resolve circumstantial tensions within the authority of self-identity.

This obsessive concern with individual identity and possibility is perhaps the key ideological feature of the emergent bourgeois self in the eighteenth and early nineteenth centuries. A visibly changeful world releases tremendous liberating energies, which, though they transform society, leave people without full control of, or access to, that world. What people are left with instead is their own privatized self-identity, which they mistake for freedom. Within the frame of such transformation, human desire and hope are real but mistaken, claiming freedom under the very conditions of its denial.[27] In *Psyche,* the ideological movement of the poem is very much in this direction, as the poem's *expression* is full of goodness, while its political unconscious carries within it the very contradictions, inconsistencies, and injustices that the poet believes have been overcome.

4.

The problems and dynamics surrounding the issue of identity—particularly the relation between identity and reification—are nowhere more evident than in the poem's handling of relations of gender. The social and historical matters traced above—the fragmentation of the modern world, the authoritative presence of commodity exchange, the struggle toward subjective identity, the desire for an unalienated existence—are at every turn mediated by the presence of Psyche, so that the poet's comments on himself and on the world are also, necessarily, comments on relations of gender within the situation described in the poem. The particular formulation of those relations energizes, in specific ways, the poet's struggle against the debilitating pressures of his world and enables him to begin constructing an autonomous identity for himself and a transcendental vision of human possibility. It is central, in other words, to the hopeful cast of the poem and therefore must be considered if the grounds of that hope are to be understood.[28]

The first social fact that must be observed with respect to gender in *Psyche* is now a commonplace in feminist criticism of romanticism and is most succinctly described by Janet Todd: "The Romantic poet's world is infinite, eternal and one, and the one, like the one of matrimony, is male. In the poetry of Wordsworth, Coleridge, Keats and even of Blake and Shelley, the female enters not usually as creating subject but as the symbol of otherness and immanence by the side of male transcendence, as a component in metaphors of reconciliation and integration, as emanation, shadow, mirror and epipsyche."[29] This is precisely the way that Psyche enters Keats's poem—as the symbolic projection of the masculine poet's dreaming ego—and it is one sign of the fragmentation and reification of human life that arise with commodity culture. While the poem purports to be about Psyche, offering a description of her in the most laudatory terms, it actually focuses most emphatically on the male poet, charting the operations of his active and shaping imagination. Throughout, Psyche is entirely passive, silent, and ideal, while the poet is active, vocal, and imaginatively industrious. The apparent idealization of Psyche becomes in fact the idealization of the poet himself.

The strategy whereby the poet elevates himself while seeming to elevate the subject of his musings discloses part of the process of masculine subject construction under the pressure of an emergent bourgeois world. It is a process that energizes the autonomous self through the paradoxical denial of self—and it is a process that can exist *only* within particular (bourgeois) hierarchal frames of reference.[30] The poem gives the impression throughout that it is the poet who is subordinate to the female figure he would worship: he is apologetic (1–4), proceeds almost as if against his will (1–4), and seems committed, in the face of all obstacles (36–37, 40–41), to singing Psyche into the ranks of the great Olympians. Each gesture and maneuver, however, calls attention to the poet himself, often in quite explicit ways. In his initial diffident expressions, for instance, it is clear that the poet, for all his timidity, is in possession of Psyche's closest thoughts and that he is sufficiently bold to set about relating them to her—"And pardon that thy secrets should be sung / Even into thine own soft-conched ear" (3–4)—even as he apologizes for doing so. Read quite literally, these lines state the poet's relation to his subject, establishing him as a benevolent though nonetheless controlling presence who alone gives voice to (and shapes the value of) her "secrets"—which of course, insofar as he controls them, are not her secrets at all but rather evidence of his determining authority.

Possession of Psyche's secrets alone, however, is insufficient to the poetic task of accomplishing the transcendence of the imagining mind. The poet ultimately claims to control and shape every dimension of his subject, and in establishing this claim he erases her character entirely, poetically casting her as a blank page to be filled with his own visions of what she should be. While she is the figure from the classical past that he most wishes to celebrate, she is poorer, in every respect, than her better-known counterparts, and in fact the poet identifies her, enthusiastically, entirely in terms of what she lacks:

... [T]emple thou has none
Nor altar heap'd with flowers;
Nor virgin-choir to make delicious moan
Upon the midnight hours;
No voice, no lute, no pipe, no incense sweet
From chain-swung censer teeming;
No shrine, no grove, no oracle, no heat
Of pale-mouth'd prophet dreaming. (28–35)

This is certainly a curious poetic expression of esteem and desire insofar as it implies that Psyche's truth, goodness, and beauty lie in her utter blankness. According to these lines, what she possesses that will be worthy of devotion will in fact be given to her, or provided for her, by the poet himself. Just as he had informed her before of her own secrets, he now lays the foundation for creating the character who possesses those secrets.

The remainder of the poem describes the ideological process whereby the poet invests Psyche with the values and features that he desires to worship in her. And here again the poetic strategy is one of apparent self-effacement that is in fact self-construction and one that (necessarily) involves the conversion of Psyche into an object. After lamenting the foibles of the modern age, including its loss of imaginative potential and spiritual integrity, the poet sets about describing the energy and labor that he will generate out of his own being and describing in vivid detail how that energy and labor will be spent in the cause of deifying Psyche. Specifically, the poet imagines himself as a "priest" (50) with a "working brain" (60); he is a spiritually devout intellectual laborer capable of creating, in his own mind, a frame that will invest Psyche with spiritual significance.[31] All of the devices of spiritual and intellectual accomplishment—"voice," "lute," "pipe," "incense sweet," "shrine," "grove," "oracle" (46–48), "branched thoughts" (52)—are compressed into his own mind as a hard crystal of individual identity. In gathering imaginative energy for the purpose of claiming—of insisting upon—his unique ability to elevate Psyche to a goddess equal to other goddesses in "Olympus' faded hierarchy," the poet brings Psyche under his own control as a way of asserting his transcendence of the fragmentation and sterilization of the world before him. The act of exalting Psyche is an act of the poet's own authority, the description of her standing as a description of his own would-be transcendental powers. On such a view, her beauty and truth lie most significantly in her consumability as an object that will quench the poet's desire to be aligned with godhead, beyond the pressures and contradictions of material circumstance.

The fairly conventional feminist explanation that I am offering here is deepened by consideration of certain class issues that distinguish Keats's poetic voice and help to clarify the specifically bourgeois character of gender relations in the poem. For even as the poem is a masculine play of authority against a wholly constructed feminine other, that authority is cast in terms of spiritualized labor, which looks forward, perhaps, to Carlyle's admonitions on the redemptive value of work. In aspiring to be a laboring priest in the service of Psyche, the poet imagines himself as unalienated and whole, fully a master of the surplus value of his labor. His "working brain" and "the gardener Fancy" (62) cultivate a rich world of intellectual and spiritual plenitude, a world in which laboring activity produces "Love" (67), human warmth, and meaningful life. Such desires, of course, are grounded in the historical reality of alienated labor and class division.

The poem's stress on labor may be seen as well as a sign of Keats's own class position. At that moment when the poet is most triumphant in his imaginings, he is still lower-class, his identity firmly set outside the domain of ruling-class leisure. And even as the poem valorizes productive labor, imagining the possibility of fulfillment in work, it duplicates the deep structure within which alienated labor under industrial capitalism is always set. In this duplication can be glimpsed the operations of bourgeois patriarchy, for even while the poet envisions himself happily laboring his way to self-fulfillment, his accomplishment is predicated upon a silent Psyche. Although he views himself in terms of his work, in fact he manages, or oversees, the installment of Psyche as an object worthy of his devotion. On this account, the surplus value that the poet enjoys comes not entirely from his own productive capacities but also from what has been denied to Psyche as an autonomous identity equal in value to the poet. Fragmentation, alienation, and reification have not been transcended but rather pushed further down into the inner recesses of social life until they are almost hidden away in one of the most basic relations of human existence—sexuality.

5.

Gender in the poem has another, more disturbing aspect. The masculine identity articulated on the surface structure arises from a much deeper pornographic, and sadeian, logic, whose modern form emerged (as I have argued) with industrial capitalism and which carries within it a need for violence against feminine existence. This is a strong expression of one kind of gender-specific operation in the poem, but it nevertheless accurately describes an important dimension of the relation between the poet and Psyche, and gender and society. For at the heart of sadeian logic, as I have argued in previous chapters, is not physical violence but rather the absolute domination of femininity by masculinity and the definition of pleasure *as domination*. At the heart of pornographic logic is a universalized masculine ego capable of inserting itself at will into any sexually desirable situation. Indeed, one dimension of romanticism might be seen as an ideal displacement of these operations.

To begin with pornography: the maneuver whereby the poet inserts his own identity into a sexual situation initiated and conducted by individuals other than himself is remarkably simple. The poet describes a scene in which he wanders (whether dreaming or awake is unclear) "thoughtlessly" (7) across a landscape of natural beauty; during his wandering he comes unexpectedly upon Cupid and Psyche, who

> lay calm-breathing on the bedded grass;
> Their arms embraced and their pinions too;
> Their lips touch'd not, but had not bade adieu,
> As if disjoined by soft-handed slumber,
> And ready still past kisses to outnumber
> At tender eye-dawn of aurorean love. (15–20)

This erotic scene constitutes the only description in the poem of Cupid, even though the Cupid-Psyche embrace is the determining event for all subsequent musings. Immediately following this description the poet erases Cupid entirely from his imagination, in one bold stroke substituting himself for the god in whose arms Psyche lies enfolded, and emphatically claiming the ability to serve Psyche in ways superior to her erstwhile lover. Such a move drains the sexual energy and excitement away from Cupid and onto the identity of the poet and at the same time establishes the poet's authority even over a god. The act of worshipping and serving Psyche is also an act of self-transcendence, achieved through the strange logic of imaginatively possessing the sexual prowess of Cupid.

The logic of pornography, as many recent studies have persuasively demonstrated, is not simply a matter of private masculine sexual desire but also a matter of power relations, as private desire is necessarily acted out in terms of other people.[32] Recognition and disclosure of these power relations were the great contributions of Sade, who surrounded his pornography with long commentaries on the philosophy of sexual relations. At the center of Sade's thought is the assumption that the active pleasure of one individual derives from the denial of pleasure to another. Among other things, Sade's philosophy discloses the tremendous sexual and cultural anxiety permeating individual life in the late eighteenth and early nineteenth centuries, an anxiety that arises with the new age of exchange value and economic scarcity and, in line with that age, takes for granted that there is not enough pleasure to go around, so that what little there is must be fought over by competing individuals. While Sade states this position in all its ugliness and mean-spiritedness, it is an attitude that is made manifest in many less disturbing—and often in quite palatable—ways during the age, occasionally even in the form of romantic desire and romantic identity construction.[33]

In *Psyche,* an idealized, or reformulated, version of sadeian logic begins to appear precisely at that moment when the poet displaces Cupid and begins to imagine himself as the "priest" most suitable for worshipping Psyche. In his initial gesture toward her, as I have shown, the poet denies Psyche an autonomous subject position (28–35) despite the fact that when he first discovers her she is happily (see line 22) wrapped in a love-embrace with Cupid and apparently without need of the poet's assistance. This denial is emphatic—no fewer than ten negative expressions appear over fewer than ten lines—and it is complemented by the poet's subsequent assertion of his own identity and pleasure. While the general celebratory tone of the poem (proceeding toward a moving pronouncement of "warm Love" [67]) may urge against a description of this relation as a relation of oppression, this in fact is what it is: the poet's desire, the poet's pleasure, the poet's need, the poet's identity, the poet's imagination—all of these appear and are shaped within the context of what the poet actively denies to Psyche, even though, in her early relation with Cupid, she is apparently an autonomous being, an agent of her own pleasure. And even if one places her within the mythic framework that casts her as helpless rather than autonomous and then reads the poet's vision as an alternative to that framework, still one cannot persuasively argue that her situation changes significantly from the classical past to the Keatsian present. Rather, she has in effect been shifted from one sort of helplessness to another; in the modern world she is made to serve the poet's desire for transcendence, even as the poet claims to be liberating her from an old system that never properly acknowledged her beauty.

It is important to call the logic of this masculinist poetic strategy *sadeian* because the word both suggests the severity of the poem's portrayal of gender and helps to link various social and cultural energies of the age within a single historical and cultural framework. The logic of the poem is not entirely under the control of Keats the poet; it is rather the cultural logic of an age, and Keats's romantic vision is constrained by that logic even as he invests it with his own particular shaping desire. While he attempts to break free of a modern age that no longer knows "happy pieties," "antique vows," and "the fond believing lyre" and to offer a vision of hope and possibility, he remains situated within the historical moment of an emergent industrial capitalism, his imagination implicated in the broad and deep controls that it would transcend. Those controls are both bourgeois and patriarchal.

6.

In *Ode to Psyche*, the past is devoured and recast as nostalgia in the poet's effort to establish himself as an autonomous identity. So the past is made to appear as a domain of infinite possibilities for the noble and loving imagination. And yet nostalgia remains tinged with the difficulties of the present, difficulties that take the form of both bourgeois alienation and patriarchal oppression. One major question that readers must therefore ask is whether the historical realities that the poem is unable to overcome fatally injure its noble expression of hope and love. The answer to this question must be that the poem's importance is not diminished but enhanced by recognition of its historical situation because the poem's yearning desire to transcend history provides an avenue into history and into the conditions of the desire for escape. Thus while the poem may not offer what Keats wished it to offer, and while its meanings may not be entirely containable within frames of reference that some modern readers might prefer, it nonetheless provides something of what historical understanding needs: an example of the controlling authority of material circumstance and of the imaginative effort to shape and direct that circumstance.

To begin reading Keats's poetry from this perspective—from the perspective, that is, of its energizing social and historical relations—is to recognize that expressive intention, textual detail and discontinuity, and reader response all carry specific, or individual, significance but are ultimately important as pressures and effects within a much larger context that is ideologically burdened and politically charged. To insist, moreover, on moving Keats's poetry away from more traditional liberal humanist frames of reference is not to deny the significance, or even beauty, of the poetry or to deny the grand contributions of liberal humanism. It is rather to reinvigorate the poetry by bringing it forward not as nostalgia but as history—as a form of visionary idealism capable of teaching valuable lessons about the past and thereby helping to inspire hope in the present for a transformed world, where beauty, compassion, and love are at last realized.

Conclusion

As several feminist studies of romanticism have argued, and as I have attempted to show in the above chapters, romantic poetry constructs masculine identity by constructing a subordinated feminine other against which masculinity can be known and measured. Marlon Ross describes this feature of romanticism perfectly in his argument that romanticism is not simply a chronological period but also a powerfully masculine ideological construct, one in which women could never function as autonomous and active agents.[1] He supports and elaborates this argument by tracing a tradition of women's writing that emerged in the late eighteenth and early nineteenth centuries to compete with romanticism and using this competing tradition as one means of exposing the specifically masculine features of romanticism. Ross's historicist argument thoroughly implicates romantic thought in the gender-specific social arrangements of the late eighteenth and early nineteenth centuries, forcing critical investigation of romanticism to explain the cultural logic and relations of gender present in romantic expressions of ideal beauty and truth.

Ross's argument is persuasive in every respect, and its scholarly thoroughness and historical intelligence help feminist analysis to understand that the competing women's poetic tradition about which Ross writes finds a voice within difficult historical circumstances only because the dominant romantic tradition and ideology against which it is set are not a monolithic cultural authority. That is, the very existence of the women's tradition that Ross traces implies that the dominant ideology of romanticism contains contradictory and vulnerable elements that render impossible the thorough suppression of other forms of writing or other ways of thinking. Even as romantic expression emerges as the shaping ideological authority of late-eighteenth- and early-nineteenth-century British culture, it harbors within its own internal dynamic self-threatening tensions ineluctably grounded in the troubled social conditions of the age. These tensions implicate romanticism in the material circumstances and social relations within which it emerges as a dominant cultural voice and—despite its particular cultural power—thereby undermine the universal claims articulated in romantic visionary idealism.

Recognizing the historical and cultural limits of romantic idealism provides a ground for understanding the importance of subjecting romanticism to materialist feminist critique. Even as a tradition of women's writing that competed with romanticism is recovered, investigated, and used as one form of leverage against masculinist romanticism, a feminist critique of the inner spaces of romanticism itself becomes necessary as a means of deepening historical understanding and intervening in the processes of historical change. A materialist feminist investigation of the complicated ideological dimensions of romantic visionary idealism not only helps to elucidate the problematic and vulnerable masculinist assumptions of romanticism—thereby helping to challenge, from within romanticism itself, romantic forms of cultural authority—but also helps to determine what elements of romanticism may (or must) be recuperated by a materialist-feminist project seeking to organize new forms of social life and cultural expression.

It is at this level of the inner historical dynamics of canonical romanticism that I have tried to enter the debate over literature and gender. If, as Ross argues, romanticism is a set of values and beliefs produced in history, then those values and beliefs necessarily register not only the triumph of one kind of cultural authority but also carry within them their dialectical opposite, in this case various (often disruptive) social assumptions that lie beneath visionary idealism as a constraining or threatening force. Particularly with respect to gender relations, it is important to investigate whether canonical romantic texts contain within their own ideological expressions of hope and desire historically and socially specific contradictions that enable the critical deconstruction and positive transformation of the masculine imagination. Just as traditional criticism, in my view, is wrong to see romantic idealism in entirely positive terms, so feminist criticism would be wrong to consider the romantic instance of gender violence as absolutely devastating to romantic expressions of hope, for such a view obscures the historical richness and complexity of romantic texts, particularly their many expressions of democratic hope and condemnations of human injustice. Put in slightly different terms, not to examine carefully the multiple and often conflicting social and historical patterns within the internal dynamics of romanticism is to risk mystifying the material determinants of romanticism and thereby to risk concluding that romanticism is *essentially* masculine, that (within a romantic formulation at least) men are *essentially* divided from women, and that men and women may encounter one another only within violent hierarchies of value and meaning. Such a conclusion, of course, would contribute nothing to a feminist project that seeks the positive transformation of masculine desire and, more broadly, the triumph of human freedom. Therefore, historicist feminist critique of romanticism must assume that, as a historical and cultural expression, romanticism can in some form be recuperated through a process of dialectical engagement.

Following these guiding assumptions, I have sought to extend the understanding of romanticism's masculinist character by focusing on the more violent aspects and underpinnings of the romantic imagination. Specifically, I have tried to show that drawing the connection between romantic texts and sadeian logic not only demonstrates, in strong terms, the possibility of recognizing the oppressive dimensions of romantic masculinist thought; more importantly, it helps to elucidate the cultural logic underpinning masculine identity—even when that identity is portrayed in sincere, palatable, and inviting terms—as well as the historical contradictions within that logic that (arguably) might enable a constructive feminist engagement with romanticism. An account of romanticism as a benevolent version of a cultural ideology grounded ultimately in sadeian hierarchies of value helps to focus not only its aggressively masculinist authority but also the kinds of potentially debilitating historical trouble that often haunts poetic expression, entrapping desire even as desire seems to command authoritatively its own destiny. Even when a poem like *Tintern Abbey* or *Nutting* powerfully articulates the triumph and strength of a masculinist ideology, it can be shown emphatically to lack the full authority that it seems to claim for itself. In fact it can be exposed as a form of expression that hides weakness as well as one that exemplifies strength. On this view, romantic desire itself is not inherently oppressive; rather, the conditions that shape and define that desire determine its particular power dynamic within culture and society.

Lynne Segal offers a general observation on the situation of pornography today that may help to clarify my view of romantic poetry and sadeian logic. Writing about the proliferation of pornography in contemporary society, Segal comments that "one very likely explanation for the increased consumption of pornography by men (apart from the significant factor of the opening up of a very highly profitable market for capital at a time when many others are closing down) is that pornography is a compensatory expression of men's *declining* power."[2] While I do not suggest that romanticism is in fact a cultural expression of masculine decline rather than triumph, I do mean to argue that romanticism reveals ideological conflict and weakness alongside its surface expressions of a confident imagination, that its strong statements demonstrating masculine identity and authority may be read as energetic efforts to compensate for loss—particularly loss of human fullness[3]—and, moreover, that the desire to overcome loss (or alienation) can be viewed as a desire for human freedom.

During the romantic period, men not only enjoyed the power and pleasure described in much romantic poetry while these were denied to women; as Sayre and Lowy show, they also felt the strong and authoritarian hand of industrial capitalism in every corner of their lives, reducing their labors to quantifiable economic activities and shaping their identities into isolatable and manageable economic units.[4] It should not be surprising, under such strong conditions, that the masculine poetic imagination of the period would often duplicate the cultural logic of capitalism, whereby desire seems unlimited but is in fact narrowly confined, and skewed by an ideology of stratification, objectification, and oppression. It should not be surprising, in other words, that romantic expressions of masculine accomplishment might also be expressions of defeat, loss, or dread that are positively recast by the dreaming power of the imagination. Recognition of this fact, I believe, is the necessary starting point for a positive feminist engagement with romanticism.

Still, it may appear disingenuous to argue that the gender-specific violence haunting romantic texts is a sign not only of strength but also of weakness, not only of oppression but also of the desire for freedom, insofar as it entraps desire and undercuts idealism. And it may appear even more disingenuous to argue that critical concentration on violence as a weakness can provide a groundwork for a feminist recuperation of romanticism. Such a line of argument seems to suggest that the romantic assault on women somehow puts romanticism on the side of the feminist struggle against domination and exploitation. But the argument is credible, and even necessary for feminist historicist critique, for at least three reasons. First, to discover the anxieties and resulting violence inherent in romantic expression is to begin constructing a vocabulary for discussing the nature of gender-specific hierarchies of value, which might encourage the construction of a strategy for their disruption and transformation. Interventionist feminism cannot simply reject violence but must account for it and for the particular energies and desires associated with it; feminism must explain the enabling logic and shaping conditions of violence if it is to be defused and its energies positively redirected. Second, critical attention to the particular gender-related contradictions surrounding romantic visionary idealism forces recognition of important social, historical, and cultural dimensions of romanticism; that is, it calls attention to the historical field where oppression takes place and, therefore, where goal-oriented materialist feminism must always begin and end. Finally, a feminist intervention that interrogates the fears, inconsistencies, and sheer contradictions that are usually mystified by romanticism's apparently brave hopes and dreams enables romanticism to be brought forward as history rather than as ideology or nostalgia, serving not only as a poetic expression of hope but also as a historical register of the real conditions of that hope. Just as Angela Carter's *Sadeian Woman* approaches sadism as a part of history and recognizes that, as a historical reality, it must be encountered rather than simply condemned if feminism is to provide a constructive intervention into unequal relations of power, so the feminist critique of romanticism must understand the historical context and dialectical possibilities of critical practice and must be guided by the positive political objective of directing romantic visionary idealism away from its dependence on gender stratification and toward the goal of individual and social justice.

As previous chapters attempt to demonstrate, and as the claims here insist, feminist critique must examine the gender violence in romantic texts, not in an effort to devastate the romantic project but rather in an effort to demystify the romantic imagination and thereby to distinguish among its various claims, betrayals, and accomplishments so that a socially and historically just assessment can begin. Such assessment, I believe, will discover that a feminist understanding of romanticism that is also *historical* cannot afford to dismiss romanticism wholesale, even if it is often characterized by gender violence, because to do so would be to dismiss as well the very real hope for human betterment that is repeatedly present in romantic idealism and that is also central to feminism. By investigating and sorting out the historically specific contradictions, weaknesses, and even horrors of the romantic imagination while at the same time acknowledging and insisting upon the integrity and human hope of one portion of the romantic imagination, a progressive, liberatory feminism may provide a new understanding of the significance of romantic visionary idealism as well as demonstrate the importance of that idealism to the feminist dream of individual freedom and social justice and equality.

Notes

Introduction

1. Curran, ed., *The Poems of Charlotte Smith;* Mellor, *Romanticism and Gender;* Ross, *The Contours of Masculine Desire;* Schapiro, *The Romantic Mother;* Langbauer, "An Early Romance"; Richardson, "Romanticism and the Colonization of the Feminine." See also Page, *Wordsworth and the Cultivation of Women;* and Gelpi, *Shelley's Goddess.*

2. Tayler, Review of Diane Long Hoeveler, *Romantic Androgyny.*

3. Sayre and Lowy, "Figures of Romantic Anticapitalism," 23–68.

4. Marx tracks this issue everywhere in his work, but for a contemporary persuasive argument about the historical dimensions of subjectivity, see Zaretsky, *Capitalism, the Family, and Personal Life,* especially 40–58. An older, cruder, but still useful explanation of romantic subjectivity is Caudwell, *Illusion and Reality,* 101–13.

5. I am drawing here, partly, on Schulte-Sasse, "The Concept of Literary Criticism in German Romanticism, 1795–1810." While my own argument departs from Schulte-Sasse's emphasis on the romantic break with the Enlightenment and attempts to locate, rather, certain intersections of romantic and Enlightenment thought, I take for granted the correctness of his argument.

For a clear statement of Schulte-Sasse's primary concern, note particularly his comment in the beginning of his essay that, during the romantic period, "the notion of a bourgeois public sphere completely relinquished its regulatory power over the practice of politics and literature. Disturbed and sensitized by the experience of a mass literary market and repelled by the development of a new bourgeois ethos grounded in economics, the Romantics retreated more and more into an aesthetic praxis, which still claimed to be socially critical but held that a meaningful social critique could be made only from the unalienated position of what proved to be an increasingly esoteric aestheticism" (99). Schulte-Sasse is

131

talking about German romanticism, but his argument applies as well to much British romanticism and particularly to a poem like *Christabel,* whose portrayal of Bracy, for example, suggests the prophetic social truth of the artist's personal vision.

6. For discussions of some of the complex continuities between Enlightenment and romantic thought, see Sebberson, "Practical Reasoning, Rhetoric, and Wordsworth's 'Preface'"; Scrivener, "Rhetoric and Context"; and Bewell, *Wordsworth and the Enlightenment.*

7. Sade's writings, including *Justine,* began to appear during the 1790s, and we know that some of the romantics—Byron, for instance—owned copies of his work. But Sade was not the only pornographic writer of the period nor the only writer dealing with the subject of pleasure in pain. A quick glance through the bibliography of Fraxi, the famous collector of pornography discussed by Steven Marcus, reveals that many of the pornographic works famous during the Victorian period were actually written and/or published during the eighteenth and early nineteenth centuries. It is probable that the Victorian boom in pornography was actually only the maturation point of a cultural phenomenon that had already established a strong foothold in the English imagination by the late eighteenth century. It is on the grounds of this historical evidence that I pose the question of the relation of romanticism to sadism.

8. Luce Irigaray, quoted in Gallop, *Thinking Through the Body,* states that Sade's work exposes "the sexuality that subtends our social order" (54). My own argument means to suggest that, if Irigaray's statement is true, *any* social reading of romanticism must contend with the ideas and logic of Sade.

9. For a general discussion of historical transformation at the structural level, see Braudel, *On History.*

Chapter One: Romanticism, Sadism, and the Question of Critical Method

1. As Praz, *The Romantic Agony,* puts it, "At a distance of only a few years— we are considering these works simply as psychological manifestations, and quite apart from any question of literary merit—there came into being Gretchen in Germany, Justine in France, in England Antonia and Agnes, in the celebrated novel by M. G. Lewis, *The Monk* (1796)" (110–11).

2. Praz, *The Romantic Agony,* 95.

3. A brief glance at the massive bibliography of pornographic literature published by Fraxi in 1868 suggests that many of the works most popular during the Victorian period, including many dealing with flagellation, were first published in the late eighteenth and early nineteenth centuries. While the literature of sexual violence against women did not become culturally pervasive until the mid-Victorian period, its foundations were laid much earlier. Pisanus Fraxi is the pseudonym of Henry Spenser Ashbee, the greatest of all Victorian pornophiles. In the 1870s and 1880s he brought out three bibliographic listings of pornographic works: *Index Librorum Prohibitorum* (1877), *Centuria Librorum Absconditorum*

(1879), and *Catena Librorum Tacendorum* (1885). These were subsequently reprinted as *Bibliography of Prohibited Books*. For a discussion of Fraxi's place in Victorian culture, see Marcus, *The Other Victorians*, 34–76.

4. Much excellent work, of course, has been carried out on the romantic gothic literature, and some work has appeared in the recent past on portrayals of romantic sexuality. But the analyses offered in most of this work have remained within the more conventional categories of romantic literary history: love, the sublime, gothic horror, and so on. A theory of romanticism's relation to sadeian logic and structures of value remains to be written. For a helpful study dealing with romanticism and sexuality, see Hagstrum, *The Romantic Body;* for an excellent brief discussion of Sade's relation to the English romantic novel, see Kiely, *The Romantic Novel in England*, 103–7.

5. In *The Romantic Agony,* Praz remarks, for instance, that "for many years the present book has been out of print, and its scarcity is responsible for many a legend. So we have happened to read in Charles Jackson's *The Outer Edges* (New York: Rinehart & Co., 1948), 185, that the 'best reading in God's world' for a sexual delinquent is supplied by 'Mario Pratz [*sic*] and Bertold Brecht.' . . . And Montague Summers . . . concluded: 'After all it does not in the least matter who is responsible for such disjointed gimcrack as *The Romantic Agony*'" (v).

6. The historical study of romanticism has been energized most significantly in recent years in McGann, *Romantic Ideology*. See also the excellent and important Lukacsian reading of romanticism in Sayre and Lowy, "Figures of Romantic Anticapitalism." For examples of historical reassessments of particular authors, see especially Liu, *Wordsworth: The Sense of History;* Chandler, *Wordsworth's Second Nature;* Butler, *Romantics, Rebels, and Reactionaries;* Scrivener, *Radical Shelley;* and Levinson, *Wordsworth's Great Period Poems*.

The feminist reassessment of romanticism has adopted numerous methodologies and pursued various intellectual and critical interests. See, for instance, Mellor, *Romanticism and Gender;* the essays collected in Mellor, ed., *Romanticism and Feminism;* Ellison, *Delicate Subjects;* Homans, *Women Writers and Poetic Identity;* Tayler and Luria, "Gender and Genre"; Ross, *The Contours of Masculine Desire;* Spivak, "Sex and History in *The Prelude* (1805): Books Nine to Thirteen"; Jacobus, *Romanticism, Writing, and Sexual Difference;* and Claridge, *Romantic Potency*. In addition, Curran is currently engaged in a major scholarly project of bringing together for publication the work of many women poets who were writing during the romantic period but have fallen into complete or near obscurity. Most recently he has edited *The Poems of Charlotte Smith*.

For an excellent and important study of pain that throws light on some of the concerns addressed in the present study, see Morris, *The Culture of Pain*.

7. The argument I am presenting here has been articulated most persuasively in McGann, *Romantic Ideology*. It has also been advanced, in rather different terms, in Siskin, *The Historicity of Romantic Discourse*. See also the essays collected in Levinson et al., *Rethinking Historicism*.

8. For a helpful discussion of romantic gothic literature in terms of gender, see the essays collected in Fleenor, ed., *The Female Gothic,* especially the essays included under the heading "Monsters—Sexuality and Terror," 167–226. See also Ellis, *The Contested Castle,* especially the chapter on Matthew Gregory Lewis, 131–50. For an excellent recent discussion of the sublime, see Arac, "The Media of Sublimity." Finally, one of the best and most comprehensive studies of the dark side of romanticism remains Bostetter, *The Romantic Ventriloquists.*

That the romantics themselves were intellectually concerned with the debilitating gap between beautiful idealisms (or at least virtue and decency) and nightmarish horror is seen clearly, for instance, in Coleridge's critique of Maturin's *Bertram* in *Biographia Literaria.*

9. For a psychological reading of the troubled romantic imagination, see Bostetter, *The Romantic Ventriloquists.* For examples of feminist criticism that remains aligned fairly closely with romantic structures of value and belief, see Lau, "Keats's Mature Goddesses," and Hoeveler, *Romantic Androgyny.*

10. See Jameson, "Criticism in History," 1:120. Note also the comment by Roland Barthes, in his *Mythologies,* that "a little formalism turns one away from History, but . . . a lot brings one back to it" (112).

11. The poststructuralist resistance to the totalizing position I am advancing here is addressed humorously in Eagleton, *Ideology,* 13.

12. McGann has discussed in helpful ways the difficult relation of the poetic text to the various contexts within which it circulates. See "The Text, the Poem, and the Problem of Historical Method."

13. Jameson, "Ideology of the Text," 1:58.

14. See Wasserman, *The Finer Tone.* See also Levinson, *Keats's Life of Allegory.* I should stress that I am not arguing on behalf of a purely—i.e., ahistorical—relativist criticism: some critical practices, in my view, are superior to others. I am simply saying that all critical strategies contain a political dimension that is sometimes acknowledged and sometimes not. For a helpful discussion of Marxism and relativism that reflects my own position, see West, *The Ethical Dimensions of Marxist Thought,* especially 4–10.

15. The presence and power of the logic of the autonomous subject are seen repeatedly not only in romantic ideological expression but also in the many attempts by romantic writers to counter the ideology of the individual subject with expressions of collective identity. Note, for instance, Hazlitt and Keats's views on the sympathetic imagination.

16. Carter, *The Sadeian Woman and the Ideology of Pornography,* 25, 119.

17. Ibid., 55.

18. Note Gallop's interesting argument, in *Thinking Through the Body,* that in Sade even age can be understood as a form of class distinction, as "age becomes the determining sign for the distinction knowledge/innocence, which is to say Phallus/receptacle" (45).

19. I am thinking here, of course, of Rossetti's brilliant portrayal of gender and

commodity in *Goblin Market*. For a discussion of these issues in the poem, see Campbell, "Of Mothers and Merchants."

20. A good, one-volume collection of Donatien-Alphonse-Francois de Sade's work is *The Complete Justine; Philosophy in the Bedroom; Eugenie deFranval, and Other Writings*. All references to Sade in the present study are taken from this edition, and page numbers are cited parenthetically in the text.

21. Dworkin, *Pornography: Men Possessing Women*, 70–100.

22. Carter, *The Sadeian Woman and the Ideology of Pornography*, 11.

23. Sayre and Lowy, "Figures of Romantic Anticapitalism," 29.

24. Ibid., 34. For an excellent discussion of the political dangers of nostalgia, see Rich, "Resisting Amnesia," 139–40.

25. Sayre and Lowy, "Figures of Romantic Anticapitalism," 39.

26. Ibid., 40.

27. Ibid., 43.

28. Ibid., 46–47.

29. Ibid., 50.

30. Ibid., 63.

31. Ibid., 29.

32. The distinction between romanticism and capitalism is perhaps drawn most clearly by Sayre and Lowy in the following passage: "The traditional intelligentsia . . . inhabits a mental universe governed by *qualitative* values, by ethical, aesthetic, religious, cultural, or political values. All of their social activity of 'spiritual production' . . . is inspired, motivated, oriented, and molded by these values, which constitute their *raison d'etre* as intellectuals. But the central characteristic of capitalism is that its functioning is entirely determined by *quantitative* values: exchange value, price, profit. There is a fundamental opposition, then, between these two worlds, an opposition that creates contradictions and conflicts" ("Figures of Romantic Anticapitalism," 63).

33. McGann's *Romantic Ideology* is the best recent attempt to theorize these social and historical mediations and their relation to romantic literature. See also Levinson, *Wordsworth's Great Period Poems*.

34. Carter, *The Sadeian Woman and the Ideology of Pornography*, 9.

35. Another way of formulating this charge against Sayre and Lowy is to say that their very effort to imagine the utopian dimensions of romanticism is necessarily ideologically burdened, controlled by assumptions that are themselves historically determined. As Jameson says (in a different context) of utopian thought: "In a fragmented social life—that is, essentially in all class societies—the political thrust of the struggle of all groups against each other can never be immediately universal." That thought "is always positioned within the social totality" (*Political Unconscious*, 283). As Carter's analysis powerfully illustrates, that totality during the late eighteenth and early nineteenth centuries was sexually violent and sexually oppressive. Sayre and Lowy's failure to recognize or to address this historical fact, as I have shown, shapes their theory in significant ways.

For an excellent discussion of these matters, see Ross, *Contours of Masculine Desire*. See also Figes, *Patriarchal Attitudes*, 92–110. Figes excoriates the work of Rousseau, which at once offers an egalitarian vision and condemns women to the role of helpmates for men.

36. Work along these lines has been initiated by Ferber, who addresses some of the omissions in the Sayre-Lowy argument.

37. Sayre and Lowy, "Figures of Romantic Anticapitalism," 62.

38. Ibid., 62.

39. Ibid., 61.

40. See Callinicos, *Against Postmodernism*, 87, for an excellent and lucid consideration of this topic.

41. My thinking about human agency has been influenced by Felski's comments on Anthony Giddens in *Beyond Feminist Aesthetics*, 55–62; Callinicos's critique of Giddens in "Anthony Giddens"; and Anderson's discussion of agency in *Arguments Within English Marxism*, 16–58.

42. For an excellent essay on dialectics and contradiction, see Meikle, "Dialectical Contradictions and Necessity," 5–36.

43. Felski, *Beyond Feminist Aesthetics*, 55–56.

44. For a discussion of patriarchy and the feminine voice in a specific romantic poem, see the chapter on Keats's *Ode on a Grecian Urn* in Watkins, *Keats's Poetry*, 104–20.

45. Felski, *Beyond Feminist Aesthetics*, 48.

46. Ibid., 53.

47. McGann, *Romantic Ideology*; Levinson, *Keats's Life of Allegory*.

48. See Ross, *Contours of Masculine Desire*, and Mellor, *Romanticism and Gender*.

Chapter Two: Wordsworth

1. Homans, *Women Writers and Poetic Identity*, 128.

2. Ross, *Contours of Masculine Desire*, 109.

3. In addition to the good feminist work (such as that by Homans and Ross) being carried out today on romantic texts, several interesting studies have also been produced on the kinds of feminism practiced during the romantic period. While these studies fall outside the scope of the present argument, two have been particularly influential on my general thinking about romanticism and feminism: Grimshaw, "Mary Wollstonecraft" and Taylor, *Eve and the New Jerusalem*.

4. Levinson, *Wordsworth's Great Period Poems*.

5. In addition to Braudel, *On History*, see Timpanaro, *On Materialism*, which, among other things, discusses the shaping authority of material conditions at an even deeper level than Braudel does.

6. For a helpful discussion, from a Marxist perspective, of the difficulty of theorizing the rise of capitalism, see the essays collected in Hilton, ed., *The Transition from Feudalism to Capitalism*. While mercantile capitalism was

established as an economic structure in England by the end of the seventeenth century, the emergence of a bourgeois worldview did not become culturally dominant (as Sayre and Lowy argue) until after the rise of industrial capitalism in the late eighteenth century. For an excellent critique of the Sayre-Lowy argument, see Ferber, "Romantic Anticapitalism."

7. This position is a commonplace in Marxist thought. See, for instance, Zaretsky, *Capitalism, the Family, and Personal Life.*

8. For a general discussion of this relation between society and subjectivity in romantic art, see Plekhanov, *Art and Social Life.*

9. My position here echoes that in Caudwell, *Illusion and Reality,* especially 101–13. Caudwell, however, never offers a systematic critical investigation of the specific social and historical dimensions of bourgeois poetry. My position also draws heavily upon the argument of Zaretsky, *Capitalism, the Family, and Personal Life,* especially 40–58, which describes the narrowing of human consciousness during the romantic period. I draw here also upon Sayre and Lowy's argument, described in chapter 1, though my position does not recognize the same sort of unproblematic utopian core to romanticism that Sayre and Lowy insist upon.

10. Several general studies develop at much greater length some of the lines of thought I am describing here. See those of Mooers, *The Making of Bourgeois Europe,* and Eisenstein, ed., *Capitalist Patriarchy and the Case for Socialist Feminism.*

11. For an excellent discussion of the historical construction of subjectivity, again see Zaretsky, *Capitalism, the Family, and Personal Life,* a work that is also extremely important for its contribution to materialist feminist theory.

12. Quotations from the *Lyrical Ballads* are taken from Butler and Green, eds., *Lyrical Ballads.* Quotations from *The Prelude* are taken from Owen, ed., *Fourteen Book "Prelude."* Quotations from the prospectus to *The Recluse* are taken from Darlington, ed., *Home at Grasmere.* Line numbers are cited parenthetically in the text.

13. For a different treatment of gender in *Tintern Abbey,* see Barrell's brilliant essay "The Uses of Dorothy: 'The Language of the Sense' in 'Tintern Abbey,'" in his *Poetry, Language, and Politics.* Barrell shows that the language of the poem is best understood "in the context of late eighteenth-century beliefs about, and attitudes to, language, and to gender: beliefs and attitudes to which Wordsworth appeals, in his implicit demand that we take his words on trust." According to Barrell, Wordsworth, as masculine voice, needs the feminine Dorothy as a force behind his own poetic vision, and thus she must be seen as a potentially autonomous identity; at the same time, her identity must be contained to assure the autonomy and authority of Wordsworth's own voice. *Tintern Abbey,* Barrell says, attempts to negotiate these two inconsistent attitudes toward Dorothy (147). Barrell's discussion differs from my own primarily in its particular attention to the relations between the language of the poem and eighteenth-century philosophies

of language; my own discussion, on the other hand, is concerned primarily with matters of ideology as they are related to forms of cultural logic and structures of violence during the romantic period.

14. This point, of course, has been made about romanticism in general in McGann, *Romantic Ideology.*

15. Barrell, "The Uses of Dorothy," in *Poetry, Language, and Politics,* 162.

16. In fact, the poet's modifying power of recollection, through which he gains access to nature in the poem, suggests that nature—no less than Dorothy—is cast as an object to be controlled. For a general discussion of Wordsworth's poetry along these lines, see Ross, "Naturalizing Gender."

17. Again, for a discussion of the *Ode on a Grecian Urn* along these lines see Watkins, *Keats's Poetry,* 104–20.

18. The ugly extreme of this attitude appears subsequently in Sade's general description of woman: "A puny creature, always inferior to man, infinitely less attractive than he, less ingenious, less wise, constructed in a disgusting manner entirely opposite to what is capable of pleasing a man, to what is able to delight him . . . a being three-quarters of her life untouchable, unwholesome, unable to satisfy her mate throughout the entire period Nature constrains her to childbearing, of a sharp turn of humor, shrill, shrewish, bitter, and thwart; a tyrant if you allow her privileges, mean, vile, and a sneak in bondage; always false, forever mischievous, constantly dangerous" (647). This passage is also cited in Charney's fine discussion of sadism, *Sexual Fiction,* 32–51.

19. Downs, *The Politics of Pornography,* 36. See also Dworkin, *Pornography: Men Possessing Women,* especially her essay on Sade, 70–100. For a useful discussion of the way in which pornography eroticizes the relation of power, see Kittay, "Pornography and the Erotics of Domination." For a helpful poststructuralist discussion of pornography, see Kappeler, *The Pornography of Representation.* For a discussion of the connections between pornography and subjective identity, see Segal, *Is the Future Female?* especially 107–16.

20. Note for instance Dworkin's comment, in *Pornography: Men Possessing Women* that "terror issues from the male, illuminates his essential nature and his basic purpose. He chooses how much to terrorize, whether terror will be a dalliance or an obsession, whether he will use it brutally or subtly" (16).

21. I am aware that the concept of nature is extremely problematic in the eighteenth and nineteenth centuries, and I do not mean to offer an explanation of the richness of that concept here. My aim is simply to suggest its use in Sade and Wordsworth as a socially unmediated origin and authority for a sort of masculinist logic that developed in the late eighteenth and early nineteenth centuries. For an excellent discussion of Wordsworth that centers around the problem of nature, see Chandler, *Wordsworth's Second Nature.*

22. For readings of alterity in the poem, see Ferguson, *Solitude and the Sublime,* 125–27, and Jones, "Interpretation in Wordsworth and the Provocation Theory of Romantic Literature."

23. My references are to the 1850 edition. While the 1799 and 1805 editions also include versions of this episode, often in very similar language, the 1850 version states more precisely the sorts of historical and gender-related matters that I wish to consider.

24. For a discussion of Wordsworth's tendency to feminize the mind in the *Prelude,* see Kabitoglou, "Problematics of Gender in the Nuptials of *The Prelude,*" 128–35.

25. Goux, *Symbolic Economies,* 203.

26. For a useful recent study of the enabling presence of the feminine in *Nutting,* see Crawford, "The Structure of the Sororal in Wordsworth's 'Nutting.'"

27. Turner, *Wordsworth: Play and Politics,* 164–67. See also Ross's excellent essay "Naturalizing Gender." Although Ross does not address the issue of imperialism, his general argument about the psychological and historical dimensions of gender in the poem is consistent with my own understanding.

28. Goux, *Symbolic Economies,* 203.

Chapter Three: Coleridge

1. I am thinking here of Arthur H. Nethercot's *The Road to Tryermaine.*

2. In a recent essay that usefully focuses the interpretative difficulties posed by *Christabel,* Galperin, "Coleridge and Critical Intervention," summarizes the poem's evasion and proliferation of meanings and its relation to critical practice: "Neither fortuitously inadvertent . . . , as deconstruction might argue, nor a tissue of contradictions, as the new historicism would maintain, Coleridgean consciousness in "Christabel," as in "The Ancient Mariner," inclines to silence not only as a measure of failure or of fear over what has been imagined, but according to the subtraction, or according to the silent ministry, which requires, indeed depends upon, the addition of writing" (63).

3. Ellison, *Delicate Subjects,* provides an excellent analysis of desire and anxiety in Coleridge's work, though she does not discuss *Christabel* at length (103–213).

4. All quotations from Coleridge's poems are taken from Ernest Hartley Coleridge, ed., *Coleridge: Poetical Works,* and line numbers are cited parenthetically in the text.

5. Cooke, *Acts of Inclusion,* 63. See also Levinson's comment, in *The Romantic Fragment Poem,* that Christabel's "curious compulsion to pray in the woods rather than the Hall associates her guilt with the moribund state of Langland Hall" (82).

6. Much has been written about the absent mother in *Christabel.* Among the best discussions are those by Rzepka, "Christabel's 'Wandering Mother' and the Discourse of the Self"; Swann, "'Christabel'"; and Durham, "The Mother Tongue."

7. For helpful discussions of the formal complexities of the poem, see Swann, "'Christabel'"; and Galperin, "Coleridge and Critical Intervention."

8. On this subject, note Swann's questions in 'Christabel'": "What is its [*Christabel's*] literary genre? But also, what genre of psychic phenomenon does the poem aspire to—is it like a dream, as we first proposed, or like a joke?" (542–43).

9. Ibid., 547.

10. Quoted in White, ed., *Collected Works of Samuel Taylor Coleridge*, 30.

11. The idea of transgression in the poem has been discussed in Galperin, "Coleridge and Critical Intervention," and in Levinson, *Romantic Fragment Poem*, 82.

12. Numerous attempts have been made to explain Geraldine's mysterious character, and I do not wish here to trace the critical history of those attempts or to engage with them in a way meant to yield yet another explanation. My aim rather is to situate her within the social context of the narrative and to comment on her function within that context. For various readings of Geraldine's character, see Delson, "The Function of Geraldine in *Christabel*"; Spatz, "The Mystery of Eros: Sexual Initiation in Coleridge's 'Christabel'"; Holstein, "Coleridge's *Christabel* as Psychodrama"; and Rand, "Geraldine."

13. For a discussion of Geraldine along these lines, see Paglia, "Christabel."

14. The character of Matilda in Lewis's *The Monk* is similar to Geraldine insofar as she too is a demonic character whose demonism is born of her absolute refusal of the codes that define the world of the story. For a discussion of Lewis's character along these lines, see Watkins, "Social Hierarchy."

15. I take for granted that the bedroom scene can be read as a lesbian sexual encounter and that the various anxieties identified with Christabel's character may be explained as a response to such a transgressive act. I also take for granted that Christabel, on some level, is both a curious and willing participant in this scene, as may be suggested by her desire, once she is in bed, to observe Geraldine:

> But through her brain of weal and woe
> So many thoughts moved to and fro,
> That vain it were her lids to close;
> So half-way from the bed she rose,
> And on her elbow did recline
> To look at the lady Geraldine. (1.239–44)

For a discussion of lesbian sexuality—and male homosexuality—in the poem, see, for instance, Flory, "Fathers and Daughters."

16. Numerous episodes in Sade's *Justine* depict the hapless heroine coming to the aid of a man in distress only to confront afterward the selfish and brutal power of that man. Note, for instance, her encounter with "Roland," a man who she discovers has been beaten by outlaws. She comes to Roland's assistance, helping him to regain his sense, only to be rewarded by being pressed into strenuous physical labor, raped, and threatened with murder.

17. Le Brun, *Sade: A Sudden Abyss*, 139.

18. Gallop, *Thinking Through the Body*, 43.

19. Le Brun, *Sade: A Sudden Abyss*, 10.

20. Ibid., 119.

21. Other critics have recognized the relations between *Christabel* and sadism, but none that I know of have discussed these relations in quite the way I am suggesting. See, for example, Bostetter, *The Romantic Ventriloquists*, 125, and Fields, *Reality's Dark Dream*, 75.

22. A passage in Sade's *Justine* represents this notion of the relation between pleasure and pain perfectly: "Is it not plain enough that the woman can share nothing with us [men] without taking something from us? and that all she makes away with must necessarily be had by her at our expense? And what then is this necessity, I ask, that a woman enjoy herself when we are enjoying ourselves? In this arrangement is there any sentiment but pride which may be flattered? And does one not savor this proud feeling in a far more piquant manner when, on the contrary, one harshly constrains this woman to abandon her quest for pleasure and to devote herself to making you alone feel it?" (603).

23. Several scholars over the years have chosen to read Geraldine's character positively, though the argument has always been hard to make. For example, note Bostetter's response to such readings: "To say that Geraldine is not a malignant being is nonsense" (*The Romantic Ventriloquists*, 126).

24. Gallop, *Thinking Through the Body*, 7. For a useful discussion of the social dimensions of the Sadeian body, see Frappier-Mazur, "The Social Body."

25. See Schulte-Sasse, "The Concept of Literary Criticism in German Romanticism, 1795–1810." His emphasis on the changing intellectual currents from the Enlightenment to the romantic periods is relevant to the point I wish to make about *Christabel*'s rejection of a bourgeois sensibility.

26. Again, see Sayre and Lowy, "Figures of Romantic Anticapitalism" and Schulte-Sasse, "The Concept of Literary Criticism in German Romanticism, 1795–1810."

27. See Zaretsky, *Capitalism, the Family, and Personal Life*, 40–58.

28. The positive features of the romantic imagination are not characterized *only* in terms of nostalgia, as is attested by such works as Shelley's *Defence of Poetry*, Godwin's *Political Justice*, and various other political documents of the period. But nostalgia is a pervasive and important feature of the romantic imagination and bears particular significance in the romantic portrayal of gender.

29. Coleridge wrestled with the problem of capitalist and precapitalist values throughout his life, as is attested often in his prose works, including his *Lay Sermons* (1816–17), *Aids to Reflection* (1825), and *Constitution of the Church and State* (1830). For a particularly interesting example of literary criticism articulating his concern that "Jacobin" values were destroying the nation, see his excoriating attack (eventually published as part of the *Biographia*) on Maturin's *Bertram*, which, according to Coleridge, spewed forth "orgasms of a sickly imagination."

30. Wallace Jackson has written very well on some of the associations between *Christabel* and the *Nightingale,* focusing particularly on a dark presence, or demonic energy, that carries over from the former poem to the latter (*The Probable and the Marvelous,* 129–31). For other, more conventional sorts of work on the poem, see Bernstein, "The Recreating Secondary Imagination in Coleridge's 'The Nightingale'"; Randel, "Coleridge and the Contentiousness of Romantic Nightingales"; and Luther, "'A Different Lore.'" A fine brief discussion of the poem in the context of Coleridge's relation to Wordsworth and in the context of romantic nature philosophy appears in Beer, *Coleridge's Poetic Intelligence,* 130–32.

31. Schulz, *The Poetic Voices of Coleridge,* 89.

32. Magnuson, *Wordsworth and Coleridge,* 143.

33. For a helpful and brief discussion of Coleridge's philosophy of mind in the poem, see Hill, *A Coleridge Companion,* which notes in the discussion of Coleridge's use of the Aeolian harp symbol to portray the mind's operations that "as Coleridge evolved the essentials of his 'dynamic philosophy' where the mind is active in perception, the Aeolian harp became progressively less adequate as a metaphor and was ultimately rejected altogether" (25). Hill is also very good in tracing the complicated composition history of the poem and showing how the various revisions reflect modifications in Coleridge's philosophy of mind (22–25).

34. See Hill, *A Coleridge Companion,* for a sketch of how the character of Sara has been variously interpreted.

35. For an excellent discussion of the imperialist dimensions of the romantic imagination, see the two recent books of John Barrell, *Poetry, Language, and Politics* and *The Infection of Thomas De Quincey.*

36. Bostetter, *The Romantic Ventriloquists,* 114–15.

37. I have written about the historical dimensions of the *Rime,* in rather different terms, in "History as Demon."

38. For an excellent discussion along rather different lines but also addressing the problem of community in the *Rime,* see Cavell, "In Quest of the Ordinary," especially 193–203.

Chapter Four: Keats

1. One of the finest investigations of the relations of Keats and history is McGann's "Keats and the Historical Method."

2. For excellent discussions of Keats's poems along these historical lines, see, for instance, Reed, "Keats and the Gregarious Advance of Intellect in *Hyperion*"; Muir, "The Meaning of *Hyperion*"; and Koch, "Politics in Keats's Poetry."

3. Studies that treat these subjects at least passingly include Murry, *Keats;* Dickstein, *Keats and His Poetry;* Ridley, *Keats's Craftsmanship;* and Mayhead, *John Keats.* See also the special issue, *Studies in Romanticism* 25 (1986), devoted to Keats and politics.

4. See, for instance, Heinzelman, "Self-Interest and the Politics of Composition in Keats's *Isabella*."

5. Because much work has been carried out in these areas of Keats studies, however, I will not focus on them but rather touch on them only in passing. See, for instance, Allott, "The *Ode to Psyche*," and Finney, *The Evolution of Keats's Poetry.*

6. While I draw somewhat different conclusions and interpret textual details quite differently, my assumptions about the relations of romanticism to the decline of aristocracy and the emergence of the bourgeoisie are heavily indebted to Caudwell, *Illusion and Reality,* especially 101–13.

7. For a discussion of the relations between this large historical context and the general body of Keats's work, see Watkins, *Keats's Poetry,* and Levinson, *Keats's Life of Allegory.*

8. All quotations from Keats's poetry are taken from Stillinger, ed., *The Poems of John Keats,* and line numbers are cited parenthetically in the text.

9. Keats scholars have long recognized that transformation is an important theme in the poem but have tended to speak of this transformation in terms of a "fall" from myth into history. See, for instance, Allott, "The *Ode to Psyche.*" See also Sperry's fine discussion in *Keats the Poet,* 249–61.

10. Eagleton has written often about the relation of imaginative writing to commodity exchange during the romantic period. See, for instance, *Function of Criticism,* 36–40; *Literary Theory,* 18–22; and *Criticism and Ideology.*

11. Marx, *Capital: A Critique of Political Economy,* 43.

12. Ibid., 54.

13. Ibid., 90.

14. According to Marx, money stands in as the universal equivalent of value, enabling all other commodities to "represent their value" (ibid., 90).

15. Ibid., 145.

16. For a useful discussion of reification in the eighteenth century within a feminist context, see Pateman, *The Disorder of Women,* 90–117. For a wide-ranging study of sexual power within the context of feminism, see Hartsock, *Money, Sex, and Power.*

17. Jameson, "Ideology of the Text," 1:52–53.

18. Caudwell, *Illusion and Reality,* 107.

19. Ibid., 108.

20. See again, for instance, the special issue, *Studies in Romanticism* 25 (1986), dedicated to Keats and politics, as well as the following: Watkins, *Keats's Poetry;* Levinson, *Keats's Life of Allegory;* Heinzelman, "Self-Interest and the Politics of Composition in Keats's *Isabella*"; and Reed, "Keats and the Gregarious Advance of Intellect in *Hyperion.*"

21. Note, for instance, the anxiety permeating the beautiful lines of *Home at Grasmere* that were later excerpted as the "Prospectus" to *The Excursion.* This

anxiety is seen not only in the poet's confessed awareness of the literary past (in the form of Milton) but also in his comment that

> ... Not Chaos, not
> The darkest pit of the lowest Erebus,
> Nor aught of blinder vacancy scooped out
> By help of dreams can breed such fear and awe
> As fall upon us often when we look
> Into our Minds, into the Mind of Man,
> My haunt and the main region of my Song.
>   (788–94 in MS. D of *Home at Grasmere*)

22. It is argued by some critics today that in our current postmodern situation, defined most emphatically by the ascendancy of the media, even the mind has been lost, as every aspect of human experience is ever more forcefully defined by, and understood in terms of, simulacra and simulations. See, for instance, Baudrillard, "Simulacra and Simulations."

23. McGann, *Romantic Ideology*, 21–31.

24. Quotations from Keats's letters are taken from Rollins, ed., *Letters of John Keats*, which is parenthetically referenced in the text, along with pertinent page numbers, as *LJK*.

25. I am not saying in the first instance that romantic poets did not write about current topics. *Don Juan* is very much about Regency England, as Graham has persuasively argued; Byron and Shelley wrote often about such topics as Napoleon or Waterloo; and Wordsworth wrote numerous occasional sonnets. But many poets, Byron included, lamented the absence of suitable contemporary subjects for serious poetry. That lament is perhaps evidenced most clearly in Byron's very funny commentary on heroes in canto 1 of *Don Juan*.

26. For intelligent discussions of the question of intention, see Weimann, *Structure and Society in Literary History;* McGann, *Critique of Modern Textual Criticism,* 65–80; and Patterson, "Intention."

27. See Jacoby, *Social Amnesia*, 113.

28. Many writers have discussed Keats's portrayal of women, goddesses, and "the feminine," though they have often done so in relatively uncritical terms (Ross is one clear exception). Among the better discussions, see Sperry, *Keats the Poet*, 101–3; Perkins, *The Quest for Permanence*, 222–23; Lau, "Keats's Mature Goddesses"; Hartman, "Reading Aright"; D'Avanzo, *Keats's Metaphors for the Poetic Imagination;* and especially Ross, *Contours of Masculine Desire*, 167–86.

29. Todd, *Feminist Literary History*, 114.

30. For a helpful discussion of specific features of bourgeois patriarchy, see, for instance, Eisenstein, ed., *Capitalist Patriarchy and the Case for Socialist Feminism*, 5–40. Among other things, Eisenstein attempts to negotiate the Marxist theory of the social relations of production and the feminist theory of the social relations of reproduction. In so doing, she addresses some of the conceptual

matters that I have addressed here—for instance, commodity production and alienation. For an excellent discussion of the privatization of women in the nineteenth century, see Wolff, *Feminine Sentences,* 12–28.

31. For a discussion of what takes place in the poet's mind in *Psyche,* see Bloom, *The Visionary Company,* 399–407.

32. For a discussion of some of the recent debates surrounding pornography, see, for instance, Downs, *The Politics of Pornography.* Although Downs concentrates primarily on issues related to the pornography ordinances in Minneapolis and Indianapolis (sponsored by Andrea Dworkin and Catherine Mackinnon), his argument includes a helpful discussion of much recent theory. See also Morris's excellent work, *The Culture of Pain.*

33. The best materialist analysis of the historical significance of Sade's thought is Carter's *Sadeian Woman,* but Gallop's *Thinking through the Body* and Le Brun's *Sade* are also indispensable to understanding Sade from a materialist perspective.

Conclusion

1. Ross, *Contours of Masculine Desire,* 3.

2. Segal, *Is the Future Female?* 107.

3. One part of this point is consistent with the argument put forward by Sayre and Lowy, "Figures of Romantic Anticapitalism" (described in chapter 1), which understands romanticism as a response to the human losses that resulted from the triumph of capitalism in the late eighteenth and early nineteenth centuries.

4. Ibid.

Works Cited

Allott, Kenneth. "The *Ode to Psyche*." In *Twentieth-Century Interpretations of Keats's Odes,* edited by Jack Stillinger, 17–31. Englewood Cliffs, N.J.: Prentice-Hall, 1968.

Anderson, Perry. *Arguments Within English Marxism.* London: Verso, 1980.

Arac, Jonathan. "The Media of Sublimity: Johnson and Lamb on *King Lear.*" *Studies in Romanticism* 26 (1987): 209–20.

Barrell, John. *The Infection of Thomas De Quincey: A Psychopathology of Imperialism.* New Haven and London: Yale University Press, 1991.

———. *Poetry, Language, and Politics.* Manchester: Manchester University Press, 1988.

Barthes, Roland. *Mythologies.* Translated by Annette Lavers. New York: Hill and Wang, 1972.

Baudrillard, Jean. "Simulacra and Simulations." In *Jean Baudrillard: Selected Writings,* edited by Mark Poster, 166–84. Stanford: Stanford University Press, 1988.

Beer, John. *Coleridge's Poetic Intelligence.* New York: Barnes and Noble, 1977.

Bernstein, Gene M. "The Recreating Secondary Imagination in Coleridge's 'The Nightingale.'" *ELH* 48 (1981): 339–50.

Bewell, Allen J. *Wordsworth and the Enlightenment: Nature, Man, and Society in the Experimental Poetry.* New Haven and London: Yale University Press, 1989.

Bloom, Harold. *The Visionary Company: A Reading of English Romantic Poetry.* 1961. Rpt., Garden City, N.Y.: Anchor-Doubleday, 1963.

Bostetter, Edward E. *The Romantic Ventriloquists: Wordsworth, Coleridge, Byron, Shelley, Keats.* Seattle and London: University of Washington Press, 1963.

Braudel, Fernand. *On History.* Translated by Sarah Matthews. Chicago and London: University of Chicago Press, 1980.

Butler, Marilyn. *Romantics, Rebels, and Reactionaries: English Literature and Its Background, 1760–1830*. Oxford: Oxford University Press, 1982.

Callinicos, Alex. *Against Postmodernism: A Marxist Critique*. New York: St. Martin's Press, 1991.

———. "Anthony Giddens: A Contemporary Critique." In *Marxist Theory*, edited by Alex Callinicos, 105–47. Oxford: Oxford University Press, 1989.

Campbell, Elizabeth. "Of Mothers and Merchants: Female Economics in Christina Rossetti's 'Goblin Market.'" *Victorian Studies* 33 (1990): 393–410.

Carter, Angela. *The Sadeian Woman and the Ideology of Pornography*. New York: Pantheon, 1978.

Caudwell, Christopher. *Illusion and Reality: A Study in the Sources of Poetry*. 1937. Rpt., New York: International Publishers, 1973.

Cavell, Stanley. "In Quest of the Ordinary: Texts of Recovery." In *Romanticism and Contemporary Criticism*, edited by Morris Eaves and Michael Fischer, 183–239. Ithaca and London: Cornell University Press, 1986.

Chandler, James K. *Wordsworth's Second Nature: A Study of the Poetry and Politics*. Chicago and London: University of Chicago Press, 1984.

Charney, Maurice. *Sexual Fiction*. London and New York: Methuen, 1981.

Claridge, Laura. *Romantic Potency: The Paradox of Desire*. Ithaca and London: Cornell University Press, 1992.

Coleridge, Samuel Taylor. *Coleridge: Poetical Works*. Edited by Ernest Hartley Coleridge. London: Oxford University Press, 1969.

———. *The Collected Works of Samuel Taylor Coleridge: Biographia Literaria, or Biographical Sketches of My Literary Life and Opinions*. Vol. 2. Edited by James Engell and W. Jackson Bate. Princeton: Princeton University Press, 1983.

———. *The Collected Works of Samuel Taylor Coleridge: Lay Sermons*. Edited by R. J. White. Princeton: Princeton University Press, 1972.

Cooke, Michael. *Acts of Inclusion: Studies Bearing on an Elementary Theory of Romanticism*. New Haven: Yale University Press, 1979.

Crawford, Rachel. "The Structure of the Sororal in Wordsworth's 'Nutting.'" *Studies in Romanticism* 31 (1992): 197–211.

D'Avanzo, Mario. *Keats's Metaphors for the Poetic Imagination*. Durham: Duke University Press, 1967.

Delson, Abe. "The Function of Geraldine in *Christabel*." *English Studies* 61 (1980): 130–41.

Dickstein, Morris. *Keats and His Poetry: A Study in Development*. Chicago and London: University of Chicago Press, 1971.

Downs, Donald Alexander. *The Politics of Pornography*. Chicago and London: University of Chicago Press, 1989.

Durham, Margery. "The Mother Tongue: *Christabel* and the Language of Love." In *The (M)other Tongue: Essays in Feminist Psychoanalytic Interpretation*, edited by Shirley Nelson Garner et al., 169–93. Ithaca: Cornell University Press, 1985.

Dworkin, Andrea. *Pornography: Men Possessing Women*. New York: Dutton, 1989.

Eagleton, Terry. *Criticism and Ideology*. London: New Left Books, 1976.

———. *The Function of Criticism: From "The Spectator" to Post-structuralism*. London: Verso, 1984.

———. *Ideology*. London: Verso, 1991.

———. *Literary Theory: An Introduction*. Minneapolis: University of Minnesota Press, 1983.

Eisenstein, Zillah R., ed. *Capitalist Patriarchy and the Case for Socialist Feminism*. New York: Monthly Review Press, 1979.

Ellis, Kate Ferguson. *The Contested Castle: Gothic Novels and the Subversion of Domestic Ideology*. Urbana and Chicago: University of Illinois Press, 1989.

Ellison, Julie. *Delicate Subjects: Romanticism, Gender, and the Ethics of Understanding*. Ithaca: Cornell University Press, 1990.

Felski, Rita. *Beyond Feminist Aesthetics: Feminist Literature and Social Change*. Cambridge, Mass.: Harvard University Press, 1989.

Ferber, Michael. "Romantic Anticapitalism: A Response to Sayre and Lowy." In *Spirits of Fire: English Romantic Writers and Contemporary Historical Methods*, edited by G. A. Rosso and Daniel P. Watkins, 69–84. Rutherford, N.J.: Fairleigh Dickinson University Press, 1990.

Ferguson, Frances. *Solitude and the Sublime*. New York and London: Routledge, 1993.

Fields, Beverly. *Reality's Dark Dream: Dejection in Coleridge*. Kent, Ohio: Kent State University Press, 1967.

Figes, Eva. *Patriarchal Attitudes: Women in Society*. 1970. Rpt., New York: Persea Books, 1986.

Finney, Claude Lee. *The Evolution of Keats's Poetry*. Vol 2. 1936. Rpt., New York: Russell and Russell, 1963.

Fleenor, Juliann E., ed. *The Female Gothic*. Montreal: Eden Press, 1983.

Flory, Wendy S. "Fathers and Daughters: Coleridge and 'Christabel.'" *Women and Literature* 3 (1975): 5–15.

Frappier-Mazur, Lucienne. "The Social Body: Disorder and Ritual in Sade's *Story of Juliette*." In *Eroticism and the Body Politic*, edited by Lynn Hunt, 131–43. Baltimore and London: Johns Hopkins University Press, 1991.

Fraxi, Pisanus [Henry Spencer Ashbee]. *Bibliography of Prohibited Books*. 3 vols. New York: Brussel, 1962.

Gallop, Jane. *Thinking Through the Body*. New York: Columbia University Press, 1988.

Galperin, William. "Coleridge and Critical Intervention." *Wordsworth Circle* 22 (1991).

Gelpi, Barbara Charlesworth. *Shelley's Goddess: Maternity, Language, Subjectivity*. New York: Oxford University Press, 1992.

Goux, Jean-Joseph. *Symbolic Economies: After Marx and Freud.* Translated by Jennifer Curtiss Gage. Ithaca: Cornell University Press, 1990.

Graham, Peter W. *Don Juan in Regency England.* Charlottesville: University Press of Virginia, 1990.

Grimshaw, Jean. "Mary Wollstonecraft and the Tensions in Feminist Philosophy." In *Socialism, Feminism, and Philosophy: A Radical Philosophy Reader,* edited by Sean Sayers and Peter Osborne, 9–26. London and New York: Routledge, 1990.

Hagstrum, Jean H. *The Romantic Body: Love and Sexuality in Keats, Wordsworth, and Blake.* Knoxville: University of Tennessee Press, 1985.

Hartman, Geoffrey. "Reading Aright: Keats's 'Ode to Psyche.'" In *Centre and Labyrinth: Essays in Honour of Northrop Frye,* edited by Eleanor Cook et al., 210–26. Toronto: University of Toronto Press, 1983.

Hartsock, Nancy C. M. *Money, Sex, and Power: Toward a Feminist Historical Materialism.* Boston: Northeastern University Press, 1985.

Heinzelman, Kurt. "Self-Interest and the Politics of Composition in Keats's *Isabella.*" *ELH* 55 (1988): 159–93.

Hill, John Spencer. *A Coleridge Companion: An Introduction to the Major Poems and the "Biographia Literaria."* New York: Macmillan, 1984.

Hilton, Rodney, ed. *The Transition from Feudalism to Capitalism.* London: Verso, 1976.

Hoeveler, Diane Long. *Romantic Androgyny: The Women Within.* University Park: Pennsylvania State University Press, 1990.

Holstein, Michael E. "Coleridge's *Christabel* as Psychodrama: Five Perspectives on the Intruder." *Wordsworth Circle* 7 (1976): 119–28.

Homans, Margaret. *Women Writers and Poetic Identity: Dorothy Wordsworth, Emily Brontë, and Emily Dickinson.* Princeton: Princeton University Press, 1980.

Jackson, Wallace. *The Probable and the Marvelous: Blake, Wordsworth, and the Eighteenth-Century Critical Tradition.* Athens: University of Georgia Press, 1978.

Jacobus, Mary. *Romanticism, Writing, and Sexual Difference: Essays on "The Prelude."* Oxford: Clarendon Press, 1989.

Jacoby, Russell. *Social Amnesia: A Critique of Conformist Psychology from Adler to Laing.* Boston: Beacon Press, 1975.

Jameson, Fredric. "Criticism in History." In *Ideologies of Theory: Essays 1971–1986,* 1:119–36. Minneapolis: University of Minnesota Press, 1988.

———. "The Ideology of the Text." In *Ideologies of Theory: Essays 1971–1986,* 1:17–71. Minneapolis: University of Minnesota Press, 1988.

———. *The Political Unconscious: Narrative as a Socially Symbolic Act.* Ithaca: Cornell University Press, 1981.

Jones, Mark. "Interpretation in Wordsworth and the Provocation Theory of Romantic Literature." *Studies in Romanticism* 30 (1991): 565–604.

Kabitoglou, E. Douka. "Problematics of Gender in the Nuptials of *The Prelude.*" *Wordsworth Circle* 19 (1988): 128–35.

Kappeler, *The Pornography of Representation.* Minneapolis: University of Minnesota Press, 1986.

"Keats and Politics." *Studies in Romanticism* 25 (1986).

Keats, John. *The Letters of John Keats.* Edited by Hyder Edward Rollins. 2 vols. Cambridge, Mass.: Harvard University Press, 1958.

———. *The Poems of John Keats.* Edited by Jack Stillinger. Cambridge, Mass.: Belknap Press of Harvard University Press, 1978.

Kiely, Robert. *The Romantic Novel in England.* Cambridge, Mass.: Harvard University Press, 1972.

Kittay, Eva Feder. "Pornography and the Erotics of Domination." In *Beyond Domination: New Perspectives on Women and Philosophy,* edited by Carol C. Gould, 145–74. Totowa, N.J.: Rowman and Allanheld, 1984.

Koch, June. "Politics in Keats's Poetry." *JEGP* 70 (1972): 491–501.

Langbauer, Laurie. "An Early Romance: Motherhood and Women's Writing in Mary Wollstonecraft's Novels." In *Romanticism and Feminism,* edited by Anne K. Mellor, 208–19. Bloomington and Indianapolis: Indiana University Press, 1988.

Lau, Beth. "Keats's Mature Goddesses." *Philological Quarterly* 63 (1984): 323–41.

Le Brun, Annie. *Sade: A Sudden Abyss.* Translated by Camille Naish. San Francisco: City Lights, 1991.

Levinson, Marjorie. *Keats's Life of Allegory: The Origins of a Style.* Oxford: Blackwell, 1988.

———. *The Romantic Fragment Poem.* Chapel Hill: University of North Carolina Press, 1986.

———. *Wordsworth's Great Period Poems.* Cambridge: Cambridge University Press, 1986.

Levinson, Marjorie, et al. *Rethinking Historicism: Critical Readings in Romantic History.* Oxford: Blackwell, 1989.

Liu, Alan. *Wordsworth: The Sense of History.* Stanford: Stanford University Press, 1989.

Luther, Susan. "'A Different Lore': Coleridge's 'The Nightingale.'" *Wordsworth Circle* 20 (1989): 91–97.

Magnuson, Paul. *Wordsworth and Coleridge.* Princeton: Princeton University Press, 1988.

Marcus, Steven. *The Other Victorians: A Study of Sexuality and Pornography in Mid-Nineteenth Century England.* New York: Basic Books, 1966.

Marx, Karl. *Capital: A Critique of Political Economy.* 1954. Rpt., Moscow: Progress Publishers, 1977.

Mayhead, Robin. *John Keats.* Cambridge: Cambridge University Press, 1967.

McGann, Jerome J. *A Critique of Modern Textual Criticism.* Chicago and London: University of Chicago Press, 1983.

———. "Keats and the Historical Method in Literary Criticism." *Modern Language Notes* 94 (1979): 988–1032.

———. *The Romantic Ideology: A Critical Investigation.* Chicago and London: University of Chicago Press, 1983.

———. "The Text, the Poem, and the Problem of Historical Method." In *The Beauty of Inflections: Literary Investigations in Historical Method and Theory,* 111–32. Oxford: Clarendon Press, 1988.

Meikle, Scott. "Dialectical Contradictions and Necessity." In *Issues in Marxist Philosophy,* vol. 1: *Dialectics and Method,* edited by John Mepham and David-Hillel Ruben. Atlantic Highlands, N.J.: Humanities Press, 1979.

Mellor Anne K. *Romanticism and Gender.* New York and London: Routledge, 1993.

———, ed. *Romanticism and Feminism.* Bloomington and Indianapolis: Indiana University Press, 1988.

Mooers, Colin. *The Making of Bourgeois Europe: Absolutism, Revolution, and the Rise of Capitalism in England, France, and Germany.* London and New York: Verso, 1991.

Morris, David B. *The Culture of Pain.* Berkeley and Los Angeles: University of California Press, 1991.

Muir, Kenneth. "The Meaning of *Hyperion.*" In *John Keats: A Reassessment,* edited by Kenneth Muir, 103–23. Liverpool: Liverpool University Press, 1969.

Murry, John Middleton. *Keats.* 1930. Revised edition, New York: Minerva Press, 1955.

Nethercot, Arthur H. *The Road to Tryermaine: A Study of the History, Background, and Purposes of Coleridge's "Christabel."* Chicago: University of Chicago Press, 1939.

Page, Judith W. *Wordsworth and the Cultivation of Women.* Berkeley and Los Angeles: University of California Press, 1994.

Paglia, Camille. "Christabel." In *Samuel Taylor Coleridge,* edited by Harold Bloom, 217–30. New York: Chelsea House, 1986.

Pateman, Carole. *The Disorder of Women: Democracy, Feminism, and Political Theory.* Stanford: Stanford University Press, 1989.

Patterson, Annabel. "Intention." In *Critical Terms for Literary Study,* edited by Frank Lentricchia and Thomas McLaughlin, 135–46. Chicago and London: University of Chicago Press, 1990.

Perkins, David. *The Quest for Permanence.* Cambridge, Mass.: Harvard University Press, 1959.

Plekhanov, G. V. *Art and Social Life.* 1957. Rpt., Moscow: Progress Publishers, 1977.

Praz, Mario. *The Romantic Agony.* Translated by Angus Davidson. 1933. Rpt., London: Oxford University Press, 1951.

Rand, Richard A. "Geraldine." In *Untying the Text: A Post-Structuralist Reader,* edited by Robert Young, 280–316. Boston: Routledge, 1981.

Randel, Fred V. "Coleridge and the Contentiousness of Romantic Nightingales." *Studies in Romanticism* 21 (1982): 33–55.

Reed, Thomas A. "Keats and the Gregarious Advance of Intellect in *Hyperion*." *ELH* 55 (1988): 195–232.

Rich, Adrienne. "Resisting Amnesia." In *Blood, Bread, and Poetry: Selected Prose, 1979–1985*, 136–55. New York and London: Norton, 1986.

Richardson, Alan. "Romanticism and the Colonization of the Feminine." In *Romanticism and Feminism*, edited by Anne K. Mellor, 13–25. Bloomington and Indianapolis: Indiana University Press, 1988.

Ridley, M. R. *Keats's Craftsmanship: A Study in Poetic Development*. 1933. Rpt., Lincoln: University of Nebraska Press, 1963.

Ross, Marlon. *The Contours of Masculine Desire: Romanticism and the Rise of Women's Poetry*. Oxford: Oxford University Press, 1989.

———. "Naturalizing Gender: Woman's Place in Wordsworth's Ideological Landscape." *ELH* 53 (1986): 391–410.

Rzepka, Charles. "Christabel's 'Wandering Mother' and the Discourse of the Self: A Lacanian Reading of Repressed Narration." *Romanticism Past and Present* 10 (1986): 17–43.

Sade, Donatien-Alphonse-Francois [Marquis] de. *The Complete Justine; Philosophy in the Bedroom; Eugenie de Franval, and Other Writings*. Translated by Richard Seaver and Austryn Wainhouse. New York: Grove Press, 1966.

Sayre, Robert, and Michael Lowy. "Figures of Romantic Anticapitalism." In *Spirits of Fire: English Romantic Writers and Contemporary Historical Methods*, edited by G. A. Rosso and Daniel P. Watkins, 23–68. Rutherford, N.J.: Fairleigh Dickinson University Press, 1990; Toronto and London: Associated University Presses, 1990.

Schapiro, Barbara. *The Romantic Mother: Narcissistic Patterns in Romantic Poetry*. Baltimore: Johns Hopkins University Press, 1983.

Schulte-Sasse, Jochen. "The Concept of Literary Criticism in German Romanticism, 1795–1810." In *A History of German Literary Criticism, 1730–1980*, edited by Peter Uwe Hohendall, 99–177. Lincoln and London: University of Nebraska Press, 1988.

Schulz, Max F. *The Poetic Voices of Coleridge: A Study of His Desire for Spontaneity and Passion for Order*. Detroit: Wayne State University Press, 1963.

Scrivener, Michael H. *Radical Shelley: The Philosophical Anarchism and Utopian Thought of Percy Bysshe Shelley*. Princeton: Princeton University Press, 1981.

———. "The Rhetoric and Context of John Thelwall's 'Memoir.'" In *Spirits of Fire: English Romantic Writers and Contemporary Historical Methods*, edited by G. A. Rosso and Daniel P. Watkins, 112–30. Rutherford, N.J.: Fairleigh Dickinson University Press, 1990; Toronto and London: Associated University Presses, 1990.

Sebberson, David. "Practical Reasoning, Rhetoric, and Wordsworth's 'Preface.'" In *Spirits of Fire: English Romantic Writers and Contemporary Historical Methods,* edited by G. A. Rosso and Daniel P. Watkins, 95–111. Rutherford, N.J.: Fairleigh Dickinson University Press, 1990; Toronto and London: Associated University Presses, 1990.

Segal, Lynne. *Is the Future Female? Troubled Thoughts on Contemporary Feminism.* New York: Peter Bedrick Books, 1987.

Siskin, Clifford. *The Historicity of Romantic Discourse.* Oxford: Oxford University Press, 1988.

Smith, Charlotte. *The Poems of Charlotte Smith.* Edited by Stuart Curran. Oxford: Oxford University Press, 1993.

Spatz, Jonas. "The Mystery of Eros: Sexual Initiation in Coleridge's 'Christabel.'" *PMLA* 90 (1975): 107–16.

Sperry, Stuart. *Keats the Poet.* Princeton: Princeton University Press, 1973.

Spivak, Gayatri Chakravorty. "Sex and History in *The Prelude* (1805): Books Nine to Thirteen." *Texas Studies in Language and Literature* (1981): 324–60.

Swann, Karen. "'Christabel': The Wandering Mother and the Enigma of Form." *Studies in Romanticism* 23 (1984): 533–53.

Tayler, Irene. Review of Diane Long Hoeveler, *Romantic Androgyny. Keats-Shelley Journal* 41 (1992): 257.

Tayler, Irene, and Gina Luria. "Gender and Genre: Women in British Romantic Literature." In *What Manner of Woman: Essays on English and American Life and Literature,* edited by Marlene Springer, 98–123. New York: New York University Press, 1977.

Taylor, Barbara. *Eve and the New Jerusalem: Socialism and Feminism in the Nineteenth Century.* New York: Virago Press, 1983.

Timpanaro, Sebastiano. *On Materialism.* London: Verso, 1976.

Todd, Janet. *Feminist Literary History.* New York: Routledge, 1988.

Turner, John. *Wordsworth: Play and Politics.* New York: St. Martin's Press, 1986.

Wasserman, Earl. *The Finer Tone: Keats's Major Poems.* 1953. Rpt., Baltimore: Johns Hopkins University Press, 1967.

Watkins, Daniel P. "History as Demon in *The Rime of the Ancient Mariner.*" *Papers on Language and Literature* 24 (1988): 23–33.

———. *Keats's Poetry and the Politics of the Imagination.* Rutherford, N.J.: Fairleigh Dickinson University Press, 1989.

———. "Social Hierarchy in Matthew Lewis's *The Monk.*" *Studies in the Novel* 18 (1986): 115–24.

Weimann, Robert. *Structure and Society in Literary History.* Baltimore: Johns Hopkins University Press, 1984.

West, Cornell. *The Ethical Dimensions of Marxist Thought.* New York: Monthly Review Press, 1991.

Wolff, Janet. *Feminine Sentences: Essays on Women and Culture.* Berkeley and Los Angeles: University of California Press, 1990.

Wordsworth, William. *The Fourteen Book "Prelude."* Edited by W. J. B. Owen. Ithaca and London: Cornell University Press, 1985.

———. *Home at Grasmere.* Edited by Beth Darlington. Ithaca: Cornell University Press, 1977.

———. *Lyrical Ballads.* Edited by James Butler and Karen Green. Ithaca: Cornell University Press, 1992.

Zaretsky, Eli. *Capitalism, the Family, and Personal Life.* 1976. Revised edition. New York: Harper and Row, 1986.

Index